This book is a monumental history of an effort inspired by the challenges articulated in the writing of cultural historian Thomas Berry. It is a testament of dedication, endurance, and tenacity, and a source book on how to create an urban eco-village like no other! ~ *Miriam Therese McGillis, cofounder of Genesis Farm, lectures and conducts workshops on Thomas Berry's New Cosmology worldwide*

I have always admired Jim and Eileen Schenk for their commitment to Earth. Now I know their story, which is more than "their" story. It is the story of a remarkably ordinary neighborhood in Cincinnati that became an urban ecovillage. This neighborhood was houses, woods, community garden plots, creatures, and humans, too, of all ages, who truly have proven that another way of life is possible even in a large metropolis in America. This may be the way many others will live, if we are lucky, as the modern world we thought had unbounded possibilities passes away. Jim Schenk is a master storyteller, and a truly honest man who brings us into intimate connection with a dream come true, warts and all. ~ *Herman Greene, Founder & President, Center for Ecozoic Studies; Thomas Berry Scholar-in-Residence, Earth Law Center*

Yay to my dear colleague Jim Schenk for putting to words so much of what I, too, have been living these past 30 years! Retrofitting urban neighborhoods into ecovillages is an incredibly challenging and rewarding life's work. I urge people, young and old, to enjoy the read, catch the inspiration, get together with a few friends, and decide on the next neighborhood to be retrofitted—maybe your own! Jim has shown that it can be done. Many of us in the process of doing it are here to help. Time is short. The changes must be rapid, and they must be deep. ~ *Lois Arkin, founder, the Los Angeles Ecovillage*

Nothing is more important in these times than finding a way to live in balance with and in support of each other and our living world. In this book, Jim Schenk provides a wonderful roadmap for how we can build communities in urban settings that honor our deepest needs to live in right relationship with our fellow humans and the more-than-human world. A much-needed treasure at a critical time in the human journey." ~ *Libby Roderick, internationally acclaimed singer/songwriter, environmental activist, poet, teacher and lifelong Alaskan*

CREATING AN URBAN ECOVILLAGE

CREATING AN URBAN ECOVILLAGE

A Model for Revitalizing Our Cities

JIM SCHENK

PINE
RUN
PRESS

Pine Run Press

For information and inquiries, please contact:
Pine Run Press
www.pinerunpress.com

PINE
RUN
PRESS

Printed in the United States of America

This book is dedicated to the residents of our ecovillage, both the human and non-human community.

CONTENTS

Map of the Ecovillage

W. Eight St.

Saint Joseph Cemetery

Enright Ave.

Terry St.

McPherson Ave.

Wells St.

ZEN

imago

CSA

The Neighborhood

1. Ice House Property
2. Jerry Ropp
3. Sharon Wilson & Dennis Coskie
4. Formerly The Bakers
5. Ken Reidel
6. Sydney Smith
7. Megan Suttman & Dan Divelbiss
8. Chris Clements
9. Deborah Jordan, Bill Cahalan,
   & Dylan Cahalan
10. Jim & Eileen Schenk
11. Suellyn Shupe
12. Matt Troken & Mary Beth McKee
13. Michael Frazier & Kim Brown

CHAPTER 1

The Need for a New Story

Our current culture needs a new story. We need to reconsider all we have been told and come to believe about the way things are and the way things have to be. Our Earth, our most important giver of resources, is exhausted, and it is imperative that we be proactive in cultivating a new culture for how we live.

Changing the foundation of our culture is not always an easy task. However, when we look at historic cultures of Native and Aboriginal peoples, we know nearly all these cultures have a completely different story about how things came to be and how they relate to the world around them. They, in addition to all of us, have an innate desire to survive, and thus all cultures' stories have evolved, adjusting to the many varied factors that contribute to our environments, from weather to types of soils, as well as the animals and plants that exist in an area or region. Each culture develops in a way to best survive in its ecosystem. And remarkably, eight billion of us now take from the resources that the Earth provides.

The Present Story in Our Culture

We have developed a system in which many people genuinely believe that economics is the primary focal point of how not only to survive, but also how to live. Our culture has been telling us that humans are producers and consumers, and the Earth is merely a resource. This underlying story has worked, as our population expansion indicates.

Making the Earth solely an extractive resource has subconsciously disconnected us from our planet. We have come to believe the Earth is here purely for our whims and we can do to it whatever we wish. This ignores the fact that we are an interdependent species of this planet, and our survival is dependent on the survival of the planet. The fact, however, is that there are limits to what and how much we can extract, such as oils, metals, and freshwaters.

Only if we see that we are totally dependent on the rest of the Earth – and begin to see this quickly – will our species thrive. This must be the root of our new story. Without the evolution of this new cultural story, our species is in danger. We, as a culture, need to protect our surroundings and help the earth sustain and grow, which in turn, helps us sustain and grow.

The Struggle

We humans have a tough time making cultural changes. We find comfort in maintaining the status quo. For example, it is difficult for the culture to reduce the use of plastic shopping bags, but why do we continue to make plastic bags that are used for a few minutes and then thrown away, especially when this material is basically going to last forever. Other prominent countries have made this switch, but the American culture is resistant because it is ingrained in our society. Even when people are aware that things are not right, it is difficult to confront and change what is widely accepted by society.

Developing a New Story in Our Cities

In developing a new story, it is imperative that we start to see our neighborhoods in our cities through a different set of lenses. No city was built with the notion or philosophy from the builders or engineers that they needed to preserve the planet. Ancient cities sprang up around waterways and trading outposts, and it is likely no one blinked an eye when garbage and excrement were tossed into the water to disappear. Modern cities may have started as relatively small enclaves of shops and services, but they exploded during the Industrial Revolution and boomed after World War II. Factories became commonplace, cars clogged the streets, and developers bought large tracts of land to build new neighborhoods of single-family homes. All these industrial notions guaranteed the purchase of lots of "stuff," which unknowingly, led to a great deal of air and water pollution and an excessive use of fossil fuels.

Most of us have bought into the notion that the Earth is here for humans, and it is simply a resource for our species; thus, all plants and animals are here for us. This notion is and was supported economically, spiritually, and culturally. It is also now spread to people throughout the world.

We need to change the way we live within our cities, but to do this, we need a new story that helps us see the Earth as sacred, and its survival needs to become our most important priority. Based on this belief, a small group of people gathered in 2004 in Cincinnati, Ohio, to form Enright Ridge Urban Ecovillage (ERUEV).

With this in mind, the Enright Ridge Urban Ecovillage has a specific focus--the city. More than half of people now live in cities. According to the World Health Organization, "The urban population in 2014 accounted for 54% of the total global population, up from 34% in 1960, and continues to grow." As such, first, we need to stay clustered in these cities or we will spread out and destroy land that is needed for agriculture, for other species, and for beauty and awe. ERUEV is working to convert a typical, existing city neighborhood to a livable, ecologically centered place. To be sustainable, we need to use the present structures and layout of already established neighborhoods in our cities. Ecologically, we cannot afford to build everything new from virgin resources. Our existing cities and neighborhoods can become wonderful, sustainable places to live.

The concept of the ecovillage is not a new one. There are many diverse and prosperous ecovillages throughout the United States and the world. However, the idea of a city ecovillage is somewhat unique. While most ecovillages are built from the ground up in rural areas, the city ecovillage takes an established neighborhood and works to retrofit it into a sustainable environment, and of these, there are few in the United States: N Street Co-housing in Davis, California; Los Angeles Ecovillage; Genesee Gardens Cohousing in Lansing, Michigan; and Enright Ridge Urban Ecovillage in Cincinnati, Ohio. These urban ecovillages are pioneers in how our culture must shift not only to accommodate the Earth, but also ensure the success of its survival.

Because we are cultural animals, our brains originally evolved in a setting where we lived, worked, and connected to people all within a space where we could walk to and return in one day. This concept of "walkable space" is what we can truly comprehend, and I might argue, what we truly desire in the hectic lives of our current culture. The urban ecovillage can offer this. We can create a community of people with similar goals who live, work, and connect within a "walkable space" – or a neighborhood.

Of course, there are challenges starting in an existing neighborhood. Most of the structures in our cities were not built based on sustainable practices. There has been, and still is, plenty of coal and gas so that it is quite inexpensive to keep our homes warm; however, both energy sources are releasing carbon in the air. Few of the houses built earlier than the 1970s had much insulation, maybe an inch or two of rock wool or similar insulation. Even though modern insulation, windows, and doors might be tighter, reducing energy consumption is still low on most people's minds. The massive homes being built today around the country – three, four, five-thousand square foot homes – is one indication of this lack of awareness.

Zoning and building codes have frequently been a detriment for ERUEV as well. In Cincinnati, growing native plants in the front yard was recently considered growing noxious weeds, and people were ticketed. Composting toilets are illegal. Any large-scale composting is illegal.

We at the ecovillage also challenge the prevailing culture with people's lawns. An urban ecovillage seeks to use lawns more effectively by planting native plants, by reducing the size of land that needs to be mowed, and by using gasless lawn mowers, thereby eliminating air pollution. Growing our own food, where our lawns were, is an integral part of the ecovillage, as is supporting local farmers and Community Supported Agriculture or CSAs. In addition, we purposely eliminate the use of fertilizers and herbicides used on lawns, which are polluting a city's water supplies.

Despite all of this, the buildings (and land around them) in Cincinnati, old and new, as in most of our cities, can be made to be ecologically sound places to live. However, it will take a group of people supporting each other to make it happen. Most people can live sustainably. ERUEV is an example of one way to do so. It is a gathering of people who are passionate about community and protecting the Earth. We are a neighborhood just like many in American cities, but together we are also proactive to protect each other and the earth, to care for each other and the earth, and to support each other and the earth. To this end, we established the following goals:

1. Create an extended family in the ecovillage. Many of us were feeling disconnected from the people around us, but we wanted to be a part of a deeper community, a stronger sense of connection. We wanted to really get to know our neighbors and feel safe. And so, when our urban ecovillage was first formed, this became a focal point in our day-to-day lives.

2. Make the shift toward prioritizing the Earth as our primary concern. The reality is we humans are just one of ten million species on the planet. Along with culture, spirituality, education and politics, economics is just one of the things that humans do. It does not need to be primary as our culture propagates. Therefore, ERUEV is looking at thinking differently about our planet. Thomas Berry, a renowned ecological author, aptly states that we are the Earth conscious of itself. Also, that our primary role is to celebrate the Earth. Our role in the ecovillage is learning how to respond to this and how to be conscious of all that surrounds us.

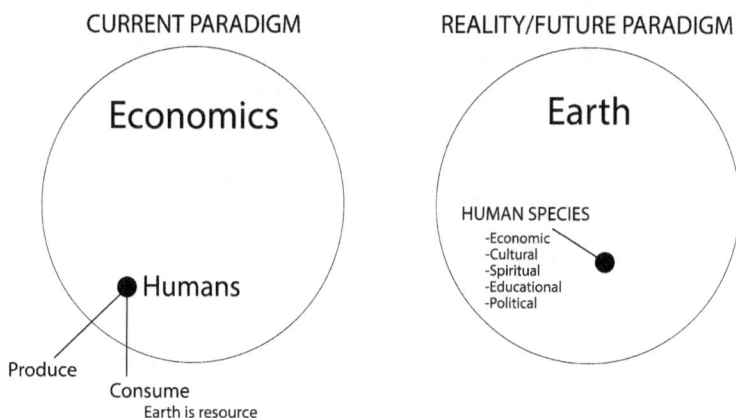

CURRENT PARADIGM

Economics

● Humans

Produce

Consume
Earth is resource

REALITY/FUTURE PARADIGM

Earth

HUMAN SPECIES
-Economic
-Cultural
-Spiritual
-Educational
-Political
●

The Roots of the Ecovillage

We are located in the Price Hill neighborhood of Cincinnati, an area housing 32,000 people where several smaller neighborhoods exist within the larger context. For the majority of its history, Price Hill has been home to working class Catholic families. In all there were six Catholic churches, and longtime residents can remember when one identified "home" by which parish church a person belonged. This also created a sense of tight-knit community. My wife, a fourth-generation resident of the neighborhood, remembers not meeting anyone who was not Catholic until she was in her twenties.

Homes in this area tend to be vintage 1900-30 and most were nicely cared for well into the new millennium. My wife, Eileen, and I moved to an apartment in Price Hill in 1972 with our first child. In 1974 we bought our house when she was 9 months pregnant with our second child. The home was built in 1905, a three-story Shotgun house on two-thirds of an acre. For the first ten years we were always working on one room or another to renovate and modernize our house.

Both Eileen and I were working as social workers in the area for different entities. In our jobs we kept seeing a recurring disconnect both between people and the Earth. In 1978, Eileen and I founded Imago on Enright Avenue in Price Hill. Imago is an ecological education organization rooted in the concept that living in harmony with the rest of the natural world is not only good for the planet, but good for us, our families and our communities. Through our preservation of urban nature, our hands-on green workshops, and our education programs for youth, Imago fosters an exciting, sustainable future that benefits us all.

Meanwhile, in 1995, city planners decided that Price Hill needed to be diversified, and when they closed two housing projects in the inner city, they directed residents of the housing project to Price

Hill. Prior to the city's initiative, home ownership was at about 60 percent. Inevitably, many people moved away from the area and housing prices plummeted, along with a decline in home ownership and property upkeep.

In response to this, Eileen wrote a proposal, through Imago, to reinvigorate the neighborhood she had witnessed decline. She received a five-year grant in 1998. In 2001 she organized a group of Price Hill movers and shakers and together they started Price Hill Will with a goal to create systemic change in Price Hill through equitable physical, civic, social, and economic development that improves the quality of life for all families in our community. Price Hill Will turned out to be a highly successful entity that continues to highlight and create programming for the larger neighborhood.

Part of the original proposal was to create an ecovillage in one neighborhood in Price hill. This was not successful because the area chosen was too large and the most economically depressed area in Price Hill; we did not have a support system there of people interested in living sustainably. However, early one morning, I realized that we could start a smaller ecovillage in our own neighborhood.

In June 2004, Eileen and I, through Imago, invited 25 families from Enright Avenue to a meeting to discuss officially forming an ecovillage and what it would look like to different people. Seventeen people came and the meeting was successful. That night we set up Enright Ridge Urban Ecovillage. The one thing we all agreed on is that we need a new story about how we live in our neighborhoods. Part of this new story is the awareness that we formed this group to develop and carry out this change. We want to be an example of how an urban neighborhood can rewrite this story. As a result of our efforts, EREUV has become a destination neighborhood where people interested in living sustainably can find the support they need to live in a closer relationship to each other and to the Earth.

My Own Story

I grew up on a small farm in Dale, Indiana. By national standards we lived below the poverty level. However, we never knew it. Before and after school on weekdays and all day on Saturdays we did chores on the farm. We grew much of our own food. While we did not have a lot of purchased or processed foods, we always had more than enough to eat. We had more than adequate clothing, much of it made by my mother. We had a six-room house, one bathroom and an outhouse, on twenty-two acres with a barn and outbuildings. We were very well taken care of. The idea that we were poor never entered our minds.

As I grew up and looked back, I realized that we lived extremely well, even though we did not have a lot. Once or twice a year, my mother would split a six-ounce Coke among the three of us. On my tenth birthday, my older brother took me to a restaurant, and I had a chocolate milkshake and got to drink the whole thing by myself. We saw this as normal, so we did not feel deprived. Possibly for these reasons, money and possessions have not been terribly important in my life.

As a young adult, husband, and father, my connection to the Earth was ineffective or half-hearted, very much part of the cultural norm. I saw it as a provider and had little conviction about protecting it or even sustaining it. In my work as a social worker, I saw that many people led unhappy lives, feeling disconnected from the people around them. Eileen had a similar regard for the Earth, and in her own work as a social worker (she worked for Catholic Charities), she saw this same disconnect that led to discontent. Together in 1978 we founded Imago. We wanted to provide a place where people could connect more deeply with one another.

Around this same time, we opened our home to Joyce Quinlan, who had just left her Catholic religious order of 39 years. She had a deep ecological passion. She greatly influenced Eileen and me to see the Earth as something that needed to be protected and revered. Through her we learned about other ecological places and people such as Findhorn Community in Scotland, Chinook Learning Center near Seattle, and the "geologeon," Thomas Berry.

And so, in 1979, with our conviction that people need deeper connections not only with each other, but with the whole Earth community, we modified Imago to become an ecological educational organization. This connected us with people who were supportive of our deep interest in Earth and of our living the lifestyle we were interested in.

While Imago has been successful and a meaningful part of my life and Cincinnati, I also discovered over the years the reality that there was not a great deal of support for living simply. The culture tells us that having stuff and money will make us happy, so if we are not happy, we just do not have enough stuff. This is the opposite of living simply. Possibly the best support system for a simple living philosophy has been Enright Ridge Urban Ecovillage.

Enright Ridge Urban Ecovillage is far from perfect, but it is a place where there is a culture that supports living with the understanding that the Earth is sacred. We do not see ourselves as a model, but rather as a living, evolving demonstration of what can be done in our city neighborhoods. Our hope is to encourage others to develop their own urban ecovillages. We understand that, learning from our successes and failures, you may do an even better job of it than we have.

While we do not claim to have all the answers to the new story, we believe we can be a part of that story. In the ecovillage, we are helping each other develop new stories.

CHAPTER 2

Community

Beginning the Ecovillage

In 1998, Imago, a nonprofit ecological education organization that Eileen and I founded in 1978, received a grant to start an ecovillage at the entrance to Price Hill. We focused on a 50-block area that we called Seminary Square Ecovillage, named for two seminaries that were formerly in the area. The ecovillage was to be formed on existing streets with existing residents.

However, Seminary Square never came to fruition. A study of this effort pointed to three things that prevented it from happening: 1) we chose the most economically depressed area in Price Hill; 2) it was too large; and 3) we did not have a strong support system in that neighborhood. We focused our energy instead in creating Price Hill Will, a comprehensive community development organization. In 2004, that organization was able to split off and become independent of Imago.

The dream of an ecovillage continued. At four a.m. one morning in June of 2004, I woke up and it struck me that Enright Avenue was not depressed, was not too large, and we had a support system of people who could help start an ecovillage. Most of us had lived on Enright Avenue for a number of years, and we had already set up relationships with each other.

We had two things already strongly rooted before forming the ecovillage: 1) Imago's Earth-centered programming had been bringing new residents to the neighborhood; 2) The residents of our neighborhood had perhaps a deeper commitment to each other already woven into the fiber of our community. Compare these two variables to the more common rural ecovillages where most residents leave everything behind; the ecovillage becomes the center of their activities, and the glue that connects them is strong. One of our challenges at ERUEV is that most people who move here come from the Cincinnati area. Because of this their commitments are in many directions; the ecovillage is just one of their areas of interest, and their level of involvement varies significantly.

In starting it, we knew that community is hard! Diana Leafe Christian, author of *Creating a Life Together*, a book about intentional communities, discusses the need to develop "glue" within an intentional community, bring people together and develop a strong commitment to each other. While an urban ecovillage can achieve community, it is more difficult than in rural ones. Typically, rural ecovillages are constructed from the ground up, developing housing settlements and community spaces that naturally create a sense of community because most residents are seeking this kind of living. Therefore, it becomes second nature. In contrast, urban ecovillages establish themselves in an already developed area, and while residents are committed to community, there are also many things to take us away or distract us, such as working outside of the neighborhood, different entertainment venues, religious practices, and extended family. Perhaps the biggest detriment is that if conflict arises, it is easy to retreat into individual homes as compared to rural ecovillages where conflict typically requires solutions.

We humans are a tribal animal, genetically oriented to community, but our culture strongly promotes individualism and moves us away from this reality. Over a hundred and fifty years ago, Alexis de Tocqueville defined individualism in the United States in this way, "Individualism is a calm and considered feeling which disposes each citizen to isolate himself from the mass of his fellows and withdraw into the circle of family and friends, with this little society formed to his taste, he gladly leaves the greater society to look after itself." This can be translated into our modern lives because many people in our culture grow up in settings where individuals, couples, or a family lives together in an isolated setting in their homes. Other people are often around us – at work, at church, at play – but in many cases we have limited interactions that do not create deep community relationships. This structure works to enhance our western industrial culture. It means that there is a better chance that people can move for a job since they are not tied down within a community. Also, it boosts our economic system where there are more housing units, and therefore, more spending on "stuff" to fill the houses that each of us own. Our culture considers this a win because it promotes independence and purchasing power.

Nuclear families are how many of us have been raised, and since we are raised in this setting, it feels most comfortable. For a communal animal and for the Earth community, it is a loss. We are isolated from each other, and our need for our own houses means resources are taken from Earth. However, our lives can be fuller when we start to purposefully develop a greater sense of connection to our community.

A Precursor to the Ecovillage

The ecovillage officially began in 2004, though several people had already moved to Enright Avenue to be part of Imago between its founding in 1978 to 2004. Imago had hosted numerous Earth-centered rituals over the years, such as celebrating the Equinox, Solstice, and Cross Quarters (they are the time between a solstice and an equinox They are commonly named Samhain, Imbolc, Beltane, and Lammas.) It also established programs such as recycling projects with kids and summer day camps and created fellowship such as small groups meeting every evening for dinner. These things all worked in our favor because this sense of community would become one of the foundations and benefits of the future ecovillage.

The neighborhood was also already doing ecological work. In the late 1980's, before recycling began in Cincinnati, we started a recycling program with the children on the street. Every other week, on a Saturday morning, we asked people to put their aluminum cans and glass in boxes on the street in front of their houses. At 10 a.m. we would take a truck with a dozen children walking alongside it and gather the recyclable materials. We would take it to a resident's backyard, dump them out, and separate them before crushing the aluminum cans. We then had dessert and drinks for the children. We sold the materials, and once a year, with the funds raised, we took the children on a trip. We went to the county fair one year, and Sunrock Farm Nature Center another year. This activity on Enright Avenue was a sign that people were beginning to think communally even then and went on for a number of years, until the city began its recycling program.

While the format of a street full of single-family households still makes up most of the ecovillage, there is a commitment to relate in a more communal way. The board of the ecovillage and its committees are one way the people relate to each other. But possibly even more significant is the support people give each other to live sustainable lifestyles along with the willingness to communicate and help each other with personal needs and tasks. People borrow tools, take care of each other's animals when away, and basically look out for each other. From meeting people on the street to knocking on a neighbor's door, to communicating through the listserv (email group), people stay in touch. In this way people who are involved because of their commitment to the ecovillage keep close contact.

The Setting

The residents in the ecovillage are closer to each other than in most neighborhoods, where frequently people do not know their neighbors at all, or only one or two of them. Pew surveys over the last decade suggest that every year Americans know less and less about their neighbors – a large change from 30 years ago, when most people in communities at least knew the names of those who lived nearby (according to a Pew national telephone survey conducted November 30 to December 27, 2009, among 2,258 Americans, including 565 reached on a cell phone). Senator Ben Sasse's new book, *Why We Hate Each Other – and How to Heal* argues that loneliness is at "epidemic proportions." Americans are richer, more informed, and more "connected" than ever, but they are also more unhappy, more isolated, and less fulfilled. The ecovillage is a way people can fight this epidemic.

Our three-quarter mile-long street that dissects the ecovillage creates an interesting phenomenon. It is not the way mindful developers would conceive of an ecovillage. Most ecovillages start building from the ground up, and in doing so, cluster the new houses. Each cluster has several houses where residents become a major support system with each other, and where other clusters are within easy walking distance. In our case it is difficult to communicate with people on a regular basis when families are three-quarters of a mile apart. When I was mumbling to an architect friend one day about the layout of the street, his response was, "You have to see everything as an asset. How do you make this setup work for you?" He suggested having stations where people could stop and interact with each other.

The early effort to section off the neighborhood into eight different segments made sense. We have around 80 households on Enright Avenue. One third of that number are committed to community and caring for the Earth, another third is open to the ecovillage activities and will get involved at times, and the other third are indifferent, but they are still our neighbors whom we treat with kindness. To create more community, we divided the street into 8 to 12 houses per segment. While these eight segments did not exactly show how residents naturally grouped themselves together in the ecovillage, it reflected the need for people to be able to come out their doors and get to know and relate to the people right around them. For example, six houses at the end of the street have formed a relationship that gives them a sense of belonging and safety. While they do not meet in an organized way, they have an informal relationship that provides them with a sense of community that has developed over the years. At the other end of the street is an apartment complex with five apartments, and the tenants have formed another support system. In another situation, a number of young families have joined together around childcare and common meals. Many of these familial relationships among neighbors helped to jumpstart the formation of the ecovillage and its mission of intentional living. Over the years, the board of the ecovillage, in collaboration with residents of the streets, decided to expand to two other, shorter streets, McPherson Avenue and Terry Street, which run alongside Enright Avenue.

One of the things that makes the ecovillage special is that while we are mere minutes from downtown Cincinnati, we also are surrounded by two hundred acres of green space and woods. The green space, mostly privately held, is in the backyards of most of our members, with Imago taking care of 40 acres. The woods consist of many hardwood trees indigenous to the Midwest like Oaks, Walnuts and Maples. Deer, raccoons, foxes, owls, many species of hawks, along with an abundant array of other birds and animals grace these woods. We recognize that it is often unusual for so many wooded acres to be situated together in an urban setting.

Some years ago, we asked each person who had part of the woods if they would allow us to run a path through their property for people in the ecovillage to use. Residents worked together to create a two-mile walking trail surrounding the ecovillage and coursing through the woods. More than the path, the woods provide people with immediate access to the other residents of the ecovillage – the non-human world. Individuals spend a great deal of time walking and exploring, and some spend time listening and communicating with the other species. It is a wonderful place to spend time. And this community of animals and plants provides a great deal of meaning to the notion of an ecological village. It is what centers us.

Makeup of the Ecovillage

When we assessed the neighborhood in 2016, there were 193 people living in the ecovillage. The following charts present the demographics by percentage of population:

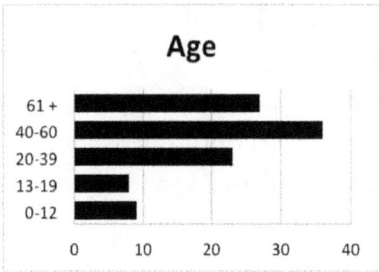

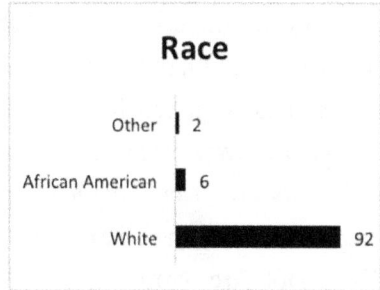

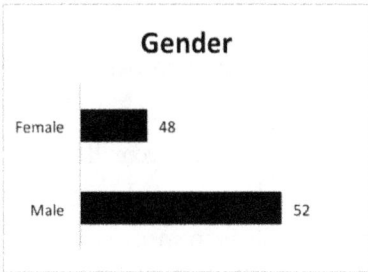

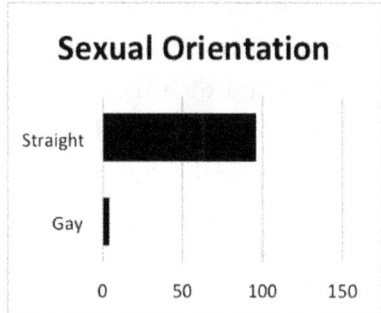

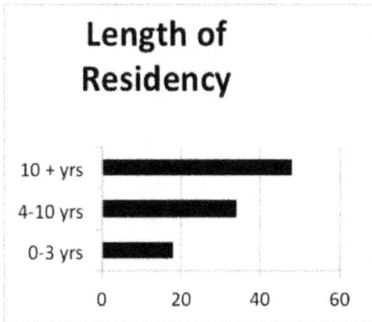

Age

Age	Value
61 +	~27
40-60	~36
20-39	~23
13-19	~8
0-12	~9

Race

Race	Value
Other	2
African American	6
White	92

Gender

Gender	Value
Female	48
Male	52

Sexual Orientation

Orientation	Value
Straight	~100
Gay	~2

Length of Residency

Length	Value
10 + yrs	~48
4-10 yrs	~33
0-3 yrs	~18

Involvement

Involvement	Value
Uninvolved	~42
Semi-involved	~24
Involved	~32

As with many organizations, there can be resistance from people who are affected by a project, but not directly involved with it. However, in our fifteen years, we have had few people in our community who oppose the ecovillage. This is mostly because this neighborhood has been cared for. Most of the houses that have been foreclosed have been renovated. The housing prices, while inexpensive, have not declined. People feel safe here, which is not true in much of Price Hill, where foreclosures are among the highest in the city. The houses in the ecovillage are maintained. People have put on new siding, freshly painted their window frames, put in new windows and doors, and overall made their homes look well kept. Because our neighbors are taking care of their homes, there is an upkeep standard that people are happy to adhere to. Foreclosures have occurred in the ecovillage, but these houses have, in most cases been purchased by Imago or the Ecovillage. We renovated them using ecological principles and then they are either sold or rented to people, most of whom were interested in being part of the ecovillage. This has helped increase the number of people involved in the ecovillage.

A significant number of young couples have moved to the ecovillage over the past seven years. These families, in most cases, have been attracted to the ecological and community aspects of the ecovillage. They help support the values of the ecovillage and expand the number of people committed to it. The majority of the ecovillage board is now made up of people who have moved here over the past seven years.

As a result of these new families, one can find children playing together out on this dead-end street or they can be found in backyards or in the Imago woods. The potlucks bring families and children together. The children bring a lively spirit to the ecovillage with their enthusiasm, creativity, and willingness to explore. These are young families who care deeply about the Earth and were looking for a way they could feel supported in the way they wanted to live, rather than feeling like oddballs in neighborhoods that did not hold these values. They have brought fresh ideas, and most of all, a great deal of energy.

Developing the Sense of Community

The ecovillage monthly newsletter, *The Ridgerunner,* is meant to keep people in the ecovillage informed about what is going on. The original organizers of the ecovillage felt that some type of communication was important so that people would be aware of what we were doing and involve them in many of the activities. The newsletter offers information about events in the ecovillage, a "gossip" column that shares observations about exciting updates in neighbors' lives, an "In Nature" column that talks about what is happening in the natural world around us, and educational pieces. It consists of four pages and offers pictures of events, nature scenes, and individuals.

The ecovillage has a board of directors that meet once a month. It presently consists of ten people: four officers who are elected each year by the membership at its November membership meeting, and six committee chairpersons who are chosen by their respective committee members.

Gathering Places

The Imago Earth Center is on 16 wooded acres with an education center, and it has an additional 21 acres farther down the avenue. People in the ecovillage walk together along the paths that meander through the Earth Center. There are frequent meetings and events held at Imago. Since Imago started the ecovillage, there remains a strong connection.

The Community Supported Agriculture greenhouse is a gathering place during the growing season. Many volunteers and shareholders come together on a daily basis, in addition to shareholders who gather each Saturday morning during its 26-week season to host a farmer's market.

The ecovillage purchased a bar, just outside its boundaries, which had been a huge nuisance. Now, it provides a center where people gather and work together. People go to the weekly potlucks held at the pub, have committee meetings, and come together for the entertainment that takes place at this site.

There are many opportunities to gather with neighbors. We have potluck dinners each week. We have had events, such as chili cook-offs, New Year's Eve parties, and the beer brewer's guild tasting parties. These events are free to join but not mandatory.

One of the gathering places many of us hope to see in the future is the purchasing of a house that could be used as a center for the ecovillage. This would be a place where people who are interested in learning more about the ecovillage could stay and try it out for a period of time. Right now, we have several people who would love to live in the ecovillage, but there is not enough available housing.

In some ways our ecovillage is much like the village I grew up in as a child, it was a small enough town that we knew almost everyone. We belonged to a Catholic church and went to a Catholic school, so we were closer to the people in the religious community. However, we were involved in many aspects of life, work, play, and so on, some of them located in town while many beyond it. One of the major differences is that while there may be a commitment to the town as community, there was not an intentional commitment to community. Unlike a small town, many have specifically moved to the Enright Ridge Urban Ecovillage with a desire to live close to others who care deeply about the Earth. Our ecovillage resembles a blend of rural ecovillages and small towns. We have a strong commitment to the Earth like other ecovillages, but also have resources, entertainment, and job possibilities right around us.

Like a small town, it is difficult to walk down the street in the ecovillage without running into someone where a conversation ensues. There are very few people who do not know each other, even among those neighbors who are not involved in the activities of the ecovillage. There are children, dogs, and so many other things going on that there is always something to talk about. The relationship to Earth and community is a frequent subject of discussion. This is the glue that holds us together.

Because Enright Avenue is a dead end, strangers often walk in the ecovillage, and because of the established collectivist culture within the ecovillage, we frequently stop to greet and get to know people as they pass on foot. At the very least, one might receive a wave from a passing driver. In addition, we rally around our community, even when the neighbors are not committed to the ecovillage's ideas. For example, someone not involved much in the ecovillage was very concerned about speeding cars coming down this straight, dead-end street. It became a place where mostly young people from other neighborhoods could drive their cars or motorcycles up and down this straight street at high speeds. Our neighbor suggested we approach the city about putting in speed humps. The community was enthusiastic about this plan and very willing to sign a petition. The city installed the speed humps, and it has significantly reduced the speeding behavior.

Another time there was an attempt to build 24 housing units at the end of Enright Avenue on a beautiful, wooded area. Not only would the community have lost this scenic area, but it would also have overtaxed the infrastructure in the neighborhood (such as water pressure), which was already fragile. The community came out as a whole to oppose this, with 50 people from Enright Avenue going to a city council meeting to oppose the development. The development was dropped. The whole community can and does act together when needed.

Sydney Smith

Sydney grew up in Louisville, Kentucky, in a family that rarely spent time in nature. She went to Northern Kentucky University where she studied public relations with a minor in Environmental Studies. There she heard about Imago and applied for an internship there in 2014. As part of her internship, she spent time in the woods at the Imago Earth Center. She didn't have a great deal of experience doing that since her family seldom went out to nature. After college she went to Colorado to learn to live off grid and live more simply. However, since they weren't vegan, she came back after four months to the ecovillage to be part of a community, to be close to nature, to be more self-sufficient, and to live a more intentional lifestyle. She was able to rent an apartment in the ecovillage and has lived there for 3 years.

Living in the ecovillage has been great for her. The first year, except for school, she didn't do much beyond her house. She had never lived alone, so working that out took time. She now has people she enjoys relating to in a shared garden space plus the large greenspace of Imago. She likes being so close to the city center, the diversity, plus having the little pocket of paradise at Imago. Her friends tell her she has something special here. She agrees and wants to share it with people.

Over the past year she has been involved in community happenings and has coordinated events. On the Imago land behind her house, she organized the building of a cob oven. She loved bringing people together to do this off grid project and get everyone's hands dirty. Afterwards she hosted an Equinox party – it was great. People love food and companionship. She enjoyed making that happen.

For her this greenspace is one of the most attractive things about the ecovillage. It is a bridge between creativity, nature, spirituality, and people: "Through it we have greenspace, fire, oven and garden right there."

One of the things that drew her here was also spirituality. It was a primary thing that drew her back from Colorado. She discovered a sense of spirituality in nature on her own. Nature is her church. However, in doing so she alienated her family in Kentucky. The ecovillage is spiritual in the same way she is. It gives her the support she would get from a family that accepted where she is spiritually.

All of this directly connects to the career she has chosen. Marie Montessori realized that we are all universal consciousness and have the same desires and needs and gets us back to our roots and away from the false projections that society puts on us. Sydney's spirituality is also supported through Montessori. The children she works with feed her own curiosity. She was an only child for 10 years and didn't have the connection of siblings close in age to explore the world around her; this career helps her relive a lost part of her childhood.

One of her goals in the ecovillage is to own one of the houses. She would also like to see a deeper love for everyone in the ecovillage and for everyone to be more connected, sharing more resources and being part of more events. She wants to see the place in her back yard to be a place where people gather and be a resource for people. She also sees Imago using it for educational purposes as well.

She's very excited about her future in the ecovillage and being part of a community she loves.

CHAPTER 3

Simplicity

For five years, my family lived on an income of $1,000 per month. We raised two children on this income. We always lived well. The basic necessities of life are not terribly expensive if one knows how to approach acquiring them. There are many opportunities to live inexpensively, such as shopping at thrift stores and growing one's own food, which make it easy to live on less without making a great deal of sacrifice.

My family grew a good deal of our food and exchanged food with others; we belonged to a food co-op and used the supermarket only when we needed to. We also canned a significant amount of our food. Having grown up on a small farm, I learned from a young age how to garden, preserve food, make bread, and cook. These were all helpful in keeping down the cost of food. We focused on making vegetarian dishes, though we were not strictly vegetarian.

We seldom had new clothes because we purchased them from secondhand stores. These stores are packed with perfectly good clothes that people discard because they have so much. Our children were some of the best dressed in their school because they could wear name brand clothes that cost us pennies. Many people feel averse to shopping in secondhand stores. The fact is people wear very few new clothes. Once an article of clothing is worn, the next time it is worn, by definition, it is "used." What is the difference if I am the one who wore them the very first time or someone else did?

We also found that there is a great deal of entertainment opportunities at universities, community theaters, and even better, in the neighborhood itself that we could take part in very cheaply. We first experienced this when I attended Case Western Reserve University; at the time we were newly married and without a great deal of money. There were so many things going on, both in and around the university, which were inexpensive. Having people over and being invited to people's homes was wonderful entertainment, with little expense. Making a large pot of spaghetti and tomato sauce was quite cheap and could feed a lot of people. We continued these practices long after we graduated, and it helped our limited income; in fact, we still follow these practices some fifty years later.

Looking at the Issue

Many people say that simple living is not simple. In many situations this can be true. It can be hard, for example, to find organic food or to grow one's food on poor soils while trying to improve it. Preserving and cooking one's own food can be time consuming. These can be challenging. However, when one looks at mainstream lifestyles, based on heavy consumption which forces people to work at jobs they hate in order to earn money necessary to continue to buy stuff, then perhaps simple living is a whole lot easier. Living simply provides people with a greater opportunity to choose the type of work they want to do. People may work part time to meet financial needs, which gives them time to do work they value. Or, following Joe Dominguez's and Vicki Robin's ideas in the book *Your Money or Your Life*, they suggest purchasing US Savings bonds because they are totally secure, and they say it is possible to live simply enough that the interest from savings can make one financially independent and able to then concentrate full time on what one loves. Or it can provide the opportunity to choose the job one really wants to do, even if it does not pay a lot. It offers many opportunities.

An ecovillage, whether it be urban or rural, puts more emphasis on simple living, which can lead to more pleasurable and happier lives. The question becomes *what makes us happy?* When the Quaker quotation of "wild beauty, peace, health, life, music and all testaments of the spirit" underlies our basic needs, then all we require are the necessities, and these take very little. For those who wish to live simply, it seems to me there are three components. The first is squaring up what one does for finances and making decisions about how much or how little one wants to consume or accumulate. The second component is happiness. This means finding those activities, events, things, and people that bring us joy and contentment. The third component is free time; living simply allows for free time to do those things that bring us happiness.

There are numerous studies that illustrate the fact that money and possessions do not make us happy. In an article in *Forbes* magazine called "Does Money Buy Happiness?" the author, Dan Seligman, says, "I'll spare you the mathematical details, but the bottom line, according to those who have studied (happiness) is that typically only 1% to 2% of people's differences in happiness is attributed to their differences in income." Therefore, it is not money that makes us happy. If "making money" is not a high priority, it frees us up to do what does make us happy.

Once we acquire the basic necessities of life, money does little for our happiness. Dolly Freed, in her book called *Possum Living: How to Live Well Without a Job and with (Almost) No Money,* makes the case that money does not make us happy. She says, "We have and get the good things of life so easily it seems silly to go to some boring, meaningless, frustrating job to get the money to buy them, yet almost everyone does. 'Earning their way in life,' they call it. 'Slavery,' I call it." So many people are unhappy with their work, but feel they need to work at a job they do not like, basically doing someone else's work. She feels this is a type of slavery. Living more simply actually frees us to do the things we love.

In the Ecovillage

We choose to be supportive of other residents if they choose not to have a "regular" job. In fact, we cheer them on to pursue doing what they love. In the ecovillage, families are exploring alternative ways of living that do not require 40 hours of work per week outside the home. An example is a family that works from home making jewelry and selling it on Etsy. They focus primarily on making rings and bracelets. I personally have given them old copper pipes that the husband cuts, flattens, and shapes into beautiful bracelets. They are both professionals but choose to do this instead. Why? Because, by establishing an urban homestead raising their own goats and chickens, they are able to stay home with their children. This is more important to them than their professions; plus, the art they produce is beautiful and allows them to express their creativity. While most of the year they are able to go to their basement and work several hours a day, the demand during holidays leads to long hours and thus requiring help from relatives and friends. People in the ecovillage support their choice and respect them for what they are doing.

Another way we are able to live simply is because housing in our ecovillage can be affordable. We live in an inner ring around downtown Cincinnati, one of many transitioning neighborhoods, where most houses are rentals. This has depressed the cost of housing, such that renovated houses are selling for between $50,000 and $90,000, but it also means that houses are inexpensive to purchase, and rentals are also reasonably priced. Furnishing the house can also be cost effective, especially when one receives furniture from others in the ecovillage, from Freecycle, Craigslist, and secondhand stores.

Transportation also offers the opportunity to simplify. Living on the bus line and only minutes from downtown Cincinnati makes the use of public transportation a possibility for many people. Being situated in the city also makes many trips short, whether going to a job, school, or shopping for needed items. When people do own cars, most of us purchase used cars, which both saves us money and often leaves less of a carbon footprint. In the ecovillage Eileen and I share our 1996 truck. We lend it out and ask borrowers to put gas in it and give us a few dollars for upkeep; it is driven around four thousand miles per year and serves many people in the community. Because very few people need to own a truck, but almost everyone has a need for one from time to time, the truck makes it easier to transport materials without having to own or rent a vehicle.

Sharing tools and other resources is a major way to live more simply and avoid duplication of materials in the ecovillage. People share their tools and equipment with each other, from rakes to rototillers. We have talked about setting up an ecovillage tool bank, though this has not yet happened. While we do not have a formal-ized system currently, there is an informal lending of tools through the ecovillage listserv.

In the ecovillage, we encourage support for insulating and making homes energy efficient because it will reduce costs in the long run by reducing high-energy bills. New technologies such as heat pumps, energy efficient furnaces, LED lights, as well as solar hot water heat-ers can be expensive upfront. Eileen and I greatly reduced our own home energy costs by installing twenty solar panels on our home. The solar panels provide 100 percent of our electric needs. Seven houses in the ecovillage now have solar panels. Home improvements like these can significantly reduce the cost of utilities as well as create more value to our time, our homes, and the earth. The ecovillage newsletter will carry stories about individuals talking about what they have done to make their homes more energy efficient. These are subtle but effective in helping people feel comfortable making their homes energy efficient.

Living simply also means finding inexpensive entertainment or creating one's own. A dog-walking group spends Sunday mornings at the Imago Earth Center where they release their dogs as they walk the paths. We now have "Open Mic Night" at the pub every week. Some great musicians play each week. One can buy a drink or just come and enjoy the music. There are six colleges and universities in Cincinnati. All of them have cheap forms of entertainment, from music to plays, to talks about sundry topics. Xavier University, for example, has a guitar series that people can attend at no cost. The University of Cincinnati Sustainability has a monthly series of environmental films, free of charge. There are community theater groups that offer plays at a very reasonable price. It is quite easy to find quality entertainment that fits a "simple living budget."

For those looking to travel, this can be done simply and affordably as well. Our family has always loved to travel. We have taken a trip or two every year since we married. When our children were home, we would pack our car, load them in the back seat and head out. Most of the time, we camped and cooked around the campfire. This significantly reduced the cost of food and lodging, making travel affordable. We usually camped in state or national parks, so we also had the opportunity to be present in the natural world. With Couchsurfing, Servas, and Airbnb, one can actually stay in homes with people all over the country and world, meaning a person can find cheap accommodations. Couch surfers have not only come to stay in the ecovillage and provided places for people to stay, but it has also brought a number of people to the ecovillage to live. I have used Servas in Australia, Ireland, Paris, and Canada; this peace organization provides homestays in 120 countries as a way for people to come to respect each other. Not only are the accommodations free, but it was also a great opportunity to meet local people in the places I visited. They were more than willing to share their knowledge about the place they live, and many would take off work and show me around their communities.

In the ecovillage, there are few accolades for owning a new car, fancy clothes, or much else that is purchased. Ours is a culture of sharing materials, tools, and skills. Residents open their homes to people visiting the ecovillage, to interns, and some offer housing for people looking to be part of the ecovillage. There is also encouragement for homeowners to make their homes ever more energy efficient, to have chickens and goats, grow a large garden, join the CSA, and install alternative energy. These are the things that people in the ecovillage recognize and support, and from which we gain a sense of comfort and satisfaction.

A lot is being written about the gift economy. It is an economy based on giving in the context of relationship rather than making transactions simply for profit or personal material gain. It recognizes that the greatest happiness comes from giving. There are so many things we can give each other, and possibly the most important is our endorsement and backing of how people are living. Because of this, residents can live in the ecovillage with ease and simplicity.

Frame of Mind

So much of living simply is a frame of mind. While the larger culture focuses on getting money and acquiring things, people often find themselves unfulfilled. However, if we develop our sense of meaning around our relationships to other people and to other species and the planet as a whole, then the mainstream consumerist lifestyle makes no sense.

The ecovillage offers a support system where living simply is not only strongly encouraged, but essential. In a culture where a person's net financial and material worth is so strongly valued, it is tremendously important to have like-minded people surrounding us. This might be one of the greatest benefits of living in an eco-village: We support each other to live in accordance with our values and fulfillment.

Living Simply: Jerry Ropp

Jerry grew up in a rural area in eastern Kentucky near Maysville. His father was not around, and his mother had a nervous break-down when he was very young. At the age of 18 months his aunt and uncle took him in on their farm. They were seriously poor. His aunt stayed at home while his uncle worked at the state highway department; during the week, the uncle lived in a rooming house. He did come home to buy food for them, so they had plenty to eat, but the rest of the money he spent on himself, on his truck, and on drink. Jerry was quiet and listened and pondered a lot. At the age of 10 he decided that someday he wanted to get out of there and move to a better place.

The farm supported them. He started farming at age 10 working primarily with his aunt. He drove the tractor and helped bring in the hay. The farm work was hard at age 10, but by 12 years of age, he was a good worker. At the end of high school in 1964 he took an aptitude test and scored high in drafting. Soon after graduation, he received a call from the unemployment office in Maysville, asking if he wanted to go to school. If he did, he needed to get there by 5p.m. that day. It was already 3:30 in the afternoon and he would have to cover 75 miles on back roads. He drove fast and arrived with ten minutes to spare. Everyone was gone but the director, the woman on the phone. She said that if he wanted to go to school to be a draftsman, the government would pay for it. He saw this as his way out and accepted the opportunity.

He went to school from 8a.m. to 2:30p.m. each day and worked at a factory from 3:30p.m. till 11:30. He would change clothes in the courthouse bathroom before going off to the factory. He received $29 a week from the government to go to school and spent that money on gas since he had to drive 36 miles each way. He would get home at midnight, sleep until 5 or 6a.m., get up to milk and feed the animals, and then go to school.

At the end of the year, he graduated and had $300 in the bank. He moved to Cincinnati, found a well-paying job, and got married. Because he was well regarded, he was offered an excellent job out of town that he turned down because his wife was in nursing school. Unfortunately, a year later, she left him. Because of this he was unable to concentrate and lost his job. To survive he started painting houses. He came to enjoy not only painting, but also rehabbing houses. He bought a house, lived on the third floor, and rented out the first and second floors to supplement his income. All of this led him to realize that he could make a living by rehabbing houses.

One day, when applying for a job rehabbing a house, he saw a paper blowing down the street. He picked it up and read a story about a person who quit his job and began training horses, a job he loved. He took a huge cut in salary, which was fine since he did not need a lot of clothing and could walk to work. The man explained that all he had to do was reduce his costs, which made it possible to do the job he loved. This is the first time Jerry thought of living simply. He realized that he was already doing this, and it gave him a new perspective. He was doing it because he *had to* but decided to change the way he was thinking. He changed his wants and needs. He no longer desired more than the things he needed.

For seven years he rehabbed houses and started saving money. He realized he could buy houses and make money. He took a course on real estate management and joined a real-estate management task group. A person from the Alternative Energy Association gave a talk at one of their meetings. The speaker said that "alternative energy was something one would do in Appalachia," which caught Jerry's interest since he grew up in Appalachia. The presenter invited them to come to an Alternative Energy Association meeting. Jerry attended the next meeting and met Sr. Paula Gonzales. Sr. Paula was a professor of biology who came to believe that we need to set up a new relationship with the planet, understanding that we are Earth. She spoke widely on this concept. At the meeting, she said, "If you want hands-on experience, we'll give it to you." This led to Jerry working for her, transforming a chicken coop into an efficient, alternative-energy home. He worked there every Saturday for five years. She talked about "live simply so others can simply live." This gave him another reason to live simply.

He met Jeanne Staas while working on Sr. Paula's chicken coop. Jeanne invited him over for dinner during the 1985 Super Bowl. They had dinner, sat on the couch, and talked. He told her the future he wanted: to live a simple and beneficial life. She said that is what she wanted too. He knew then that he wanted to marry her. They had a respectful, mature love, not a strong romantic love. They just fit together. They wanted to live a fulfilled and meaningful life together.

Later that year they saw a house on Enright Avenue and bought it. They got married on June 9 and moved in. He put into action what he learned from Sr. Paula. He super-insulated their house by adding another layer of insulation around the outside of the house, framing it out with 2"X4" s. Their utility bill was $24 per month with an air-conditioner and freezer. They had a wood-burning stove for heat. They used about a half cord of wood per year. The first year, someone paid him to cut down a tree. He used the wood for heat. Since then, he has found different ways of acquiring free wood, using pallets, trees he cuts for other people and other wood he "came by." Jerry would get the wood, and Jeanne would build a fire, which she could do in minutes. She said she was not warm in her life until they got the wood-burning stove.

The two of them always did little things for each other. They worked together a lot. He would dig potatoes, and she loved picking them up. She helped him insulate at least twenty-five houses, which they loved doing because of what it would do for the environment. It was comfort and love all in one.

Jerry learned how to invest, first in real estate through the Veterans Administration. He had nine housing units with a positive cash flow, and he rehabbed houses. Each year Jeanne contributed $25,000 from her nurse's salary, they got $25,000 from rentals, and he made $25,000 rehabbing. Because they lived simply, they were able to invest $50,000 per year at 18 percent interest. Over the years they became financially independent and could have quit working at any time. They continued working because they believed in what they were doing.

After moving to Enright Avenue, they became involved with Imago and later with the ecovillage and met some great people. What Imago and the ecovillage were doing was very much the same as they were doing. They owned four houses on Enright Avenue as a way to support the growth of the neighborhood. People in the community supported this and so much of what they did. Many of our ecovillage members have houses that Jerry worked on, including Deborah Jordan, and Michael Frasier and Kim Brown.

Jeanne died in 2013. She continued her part-time nursing job until just months before she died because she loved doing it. It has been a struggle for Jerry to live without her. People in the ecovillage have been a help in his continuing on. Rehabbing additional houses in the ecovillage has helped in keeping him busy. He has no desire to change the lifestyle they developed. He enjoys the opportunity to help others out financially, since he has the resources to do so. He fully plans to stay in the ecovillage. It is his home.

CHAPTER 4

Making Decisions and Structuring an Organization

In the Beginning

Imago provided the guiding force in the formation of the ecovillage. As director of Imago, I saw developing an ecovillage in the neighborhood where it was located as a way to walk our talk. When we all got together for the initial meeting, we divided into three groups and spent the evening answering these questions:

- What does an ecovillage mean to me?
- What would it mean on Enright Avenue?
- What would an ecovillage look like on Enright Avenue?

All organizations have to start with people choosing how to make an idea a reality. When an ecovillage starts from scratch, the group must make decisions about where to build, what it will look like, and how to structure the space. Many ecovillages never get off the ground because the sheer amount of decision making is too much, not to mention the huge financial investment that is needed. These were not issues for our retrofit ecovillage.

On the first night we met, our first decision was simply to be an ecovillage, and the next was what to name it. Because our neighborhood is on a ridge and because we are urban, we easily decided on the name, Enright Ridge Urban Ecovillage (ERUEV). The ecovillage was in an existing neighborhood, so we did not have to worry about building new homes or working out the infrastructure. Instead, we were able to think of other more achievable goals we could aim for and projects we could take on immediately.

We formed committees around these projects and decided to tackle things like hiking trails, a community building (for outreach, events, meals, etc.), skill sharing, and defining the boundaries of the ecovillage. We gave the committees authority to make decisions in the areas they took responsibility for, though we required any decisions that would need funds to come back to the group for authorization. To begin, Imago provided some seed money for the ecovillage.

To fortify the structure of the young organization, I volunteered to be the part-time staff person since I was already working through Imago. We also hired an AmeriCorps person who worked with me extensively on organizing the committees and helping them carry out their tasks. While we helped guide the different committees, all the official decisions were made using consensus by those who attended the meetings.

As the first round of committees worked through their projects, we saw what was possible, what would be difficult, and how time, energy, money, and labor can all be limiting factors to different degrees. One committee set out to mark the entrance of the ecovillage to impart some unity. They received approval from the large group about using flowerpots that would bear the name, and they assembled them from materials and donated funds from members.

While some committees, such as those in charge of the entrance, those tackling the hiking trails, and those setting up regular community meals, completed their tasks, some of the other committees ran out of steam. For example, the skill-sharing committee never really materialized. People, of course, shared skills, but this committee did not develop a formal method or database to help circulate this information.

Even when a project was not accomplished right away, if the idea was good, it tended to come up again. The momentum of our larger group did not slow down even when some projects fizzled out. Instead, we focused on things that we saw a more immediate need for; this helped turn us into a more official organization. We set up a steering committee on a temporary basis to deal with establishing the core structure of the ecovillage to work on the following:

- Developing a Vision Statement and Mission Statement
- Welcoming new people moving into the ecovillage
- Reaching out to other people in the ecovillage
- Creating a brochure

Involving the Whole Community

Involving the rest of the residents living in the ecovillage took on a high priority. Members of the steering committee produced a newsletter and passed it out. It began as an irregular advertisement for events like "Coffee, Dessert and Conversation." It grew into a monthly publication that included upcoming events, happenings in the ecovillage, educational pieces, and introducing new residents of the ecovillage. The newsletter is still published and distributed to everyone living in the ecovillage neighborhood.

In order to receive more feedback about priorities and concerns from all of the neighbors, someone suggested doing a "Treasure

Map" on the street. The treasure map was a collage that asked people what they would like to see in the ecovillage. A four-foot by four-foot box was formed with four pieces of plywood. On top of each side was written: "What would you like to see in the ecovillage around..." and each side had a different goal: Family, Greening, Housing, and Marketing. On October 1, 2005, we took the collage to eight different locations in the ecovillage and at each location neighbors were invited to add their thoughts, ideas and vision for Enright Ridge Urban Ecovillage. Two-thirds of the households added their opinions to the boards and, based on their input, we formed new committees:

- **The Housing Committee** purchased houses, first using loans from Imago members, and then we discovered a foundation that would lend us the money to purchase and rehab houses. We only acquired houses that were foreclosed on or for whatever reason would be susceptible to being purchased by investors who would use them as rentals to generate income. This troubled us, however, as investors often had no real concern for the community. We purchased these houses when we could. They were usually in very bad shape; we would rehab them by making them as energy efficient as possible and sell them to homeowners at close to cost. In most cases they were sold to people interested in being part of the ecovillage.
- **Environmental Green Group (EGG)** focused on encouraging people in the ecovillage to live as green as possible. They gave ideas for insulating homes, provided workshops on solar energy, started rain gardens, forest gardens, and the like.
- **The Promotions Committee** focused on marketing the ecovillage. They gave talks to groups and schools in the area and organized a housing tour of the ecovillage. They also

marketed the houses available as a way to bring people into the ecovillage.

- **The Communications Committee** focused on educating people within the ecovillage and beyond to live more sustainably. They put out the monthly newsletter, set up a website, gave presentations about the ecovillage to clubs and universities, and published articles about the ecovillage in local and regional publications.

Reaching Independence

It took more than a year for the IRS to approve the ecovillage's 501(c) (3) tax-exempt status. It finally came through in September of 2007. This new entity brought about a change in structure. The steering committee created a board for the ecovillage; those who lived in the community and officially joined the ecovillage could run for one-year officer positions. The board elected the first officers at the November board meeting, to start in January 2008. The rest of the board was made up of all residents who became paying members of the ecovillage. At this point the ecovillage became its own organization separate from Imago. This meant that there was no longer a need to receive approval from Imago to proceed on a project or for expenditures.

The board chose to continue the consensus-based decision-making model. However, if a decision was necessary on a proposal and someone was blocking it, the board, with a three-quarters majority, could decide to vote on the proposal. If voting on an issue was passed, it then took a two-thirds majority for the proposal to be approved. In its years of existence there has been only one block of a decision.

Transitioning

In 2008, we experienced a change regarding responsibilities among some members that resulted in concern about finances. There was also a drop-off in attendance for the board meetings, which suggested that members did not feel a strong need to be involved with them. This is sometimes a by-product of living in an urban ecovillage. People generally have lives in the city – jobs, church, family, etc. – when they move here. While the ecovillage provides them with a great deal of support in living sustainably, the ecovillage as an organization can fall low on their priority list.

Some members grew concerned that there was not enough transparency with the finances and with the work that was being done by the committees. The staff from Imago was singled out because they were working nearly full-time and making a lot of decisions. The ecovillage had reached a point where its members could and wanted to take over more of the day-to-day responsibilities. It was a transition that needed to take place, and so the Imago staff officially stepped down and made room for the residents to step up and own the organization more fully.

The members amended the by-laws of the ecovillage to reflect this change and the board became representative. The members, at the annual November membership meeting, elected the officers, and the chairpersons of the committees made up the rest of the board.

This structural change caused some temporary difficulties in 2010. In that year there were only five board members because several had resigned, and the board struggled to accomplish anything, while turning to the question as to whether or not the organization should continue. The board ultimately made the decision to push through and focus on the successes of some of the committees, relying on the momentum from those endeavors.

A New Beginning

With 2011 came a new group of board members committed to working together. They put in place some long-term structural changes, such as a yearly retreat for the board to plan for the year ahead, and they developed a manual that would help new board members understand their responsibilities. They made a real effort to become a solid, decision-making organization.

This newfound commitment enticed new officers who had little previous involvement in the running of the ecovillage but brought a great deal of enthusiasm. They started out focusing their energy on making all the systems work more efficiently. New enthusiasm combined with input from long-time members of the board formed a rational approach to systematic improvement.

The ecovillage's CSA, which began during the chaos of 2009, had become a central program of the ecovillage. The Communications and Ecovillage Green Group (EGG) committees continued to function and carry out their tasks.

The Housing Committee, lacking strong leadership, deteriorated to a one-person responsibility. This led to some major inefficiency and a decrease in income from housing, which was one of the major sources of operation funds for the ecovillage. This made things a little tight financially.

Through it all, we strived to give everyone a sense of openness and responsibility to what it means to be part of the community, particularly a leading part. It is a strength of our ecovillage that we have well-rooted residents in conversation with those who are new and eager to be in our soil. Currently, the ecovillage board is looking to learn and work from the lessons of Diana Leafe Christian and her ideas about "Decision Making in a Sustainable Community" and "Sociocracy."

It is not unusual for an organization to go through growing pains. It frequently takes stick-to-itiveness to get through this period. Enright Ridge Urban Ecovillage continues as an organization because enough people felt it was a worthwhile undertaking and were willing to work through a challenging situation. This points to the difficulty of learning to live in community but also to the strong desire for community among the members of the ecovillage. As a whole, the community is functioning well together; decisions continue to be made and the ecovillage continues to grow, experiencing new levels of progress each step of the way.

Decision Making: Deborah Jordan

Deborah has been intrigued by alternative communities since the 70's when she lived in a variety of group households from urban Washington, DC to rural Athens, Ohio, to urban and rural Cincinnati, Ohio.

One of her formative learning and living experiments occurred in a communal household fondly named Southern Rainbow in the South Avondale neighborhood of Cincinnati. The household consisted of nine people who owned the house together, shared rotating jobs including cooking nightly dinners, and met for regular house meetings to build community and make decisions. The level of connection and intentionality were high, and, of course, there was also occasional conflict. This experience educated her in consensus decision making as they took turns facilitating meetings and practiced constructive criticism using reflective listening and "I messages." They also had a lot of fun.

She moved to Enright Avenue in 1986 to live with Jim and Eileen Schenk "temporarily." She eventually met her husband, Bill Cahalan, and they decided to take root here on the ridge growing a life and a family. They felt fortunate that ERUEV took off in their own backyard. In retrospect, she feels that the development of the ecovillage in this seemingly ordinary neighborhood was a natural and intentional outgrowth of Imago, the Schenks, and all the rest of the people involved.

When the nonprofit was formed and decisions on structural issues were being made, Deborah was one of those who advocated for using the consensus process to fit her vision of an ecovillage. She never cared for Robert's Rules of Order, remembering with distaste a community council meeting where people kept saying "point of order" and calling for a vote. If much of the rest of the structure and bylaws of the ecovillage nonprofit were conventional, at least decision making could be more cooperative. She even offered several trainings in this process for those who were not familiar with it. Training and practice are important in any form of group decision making.

Consensus can be difficult to understand as a result of the individualistic mainstream society where differences are dealt with in terms of majority rule. With consensus, there is an underlying belief that each person has something to contribute to the group, and better decisions can be crafted when everyone collaborates. Consensus embodies "power with" rather than "power over" and this means a win-win or at least fair-fair structure.

Because of Deborah's experience with consensus and facilitation, she agreed to be the first Board president. We chose this title purely because it was required as part of our nonprofit status. She served twice in that capacity. During her first term of service, she saw her role as a facilitator for meetings, but it became more about practicing diplomacy. As a forming organization, we had the usual difficulty and adventure of "flying by the seat of one's pants" in uncharted territory. Some of the challenges included the following:

- Understanding and naming the difficulties in this uncharted territory: We were defining our connection with Imago, and we also were figuring out how employees who worked both for Imago and Enright Ridge Urban Ecovillage would split their time between the two organizations. Most ecovillage members were volunteers, putting in fewer hours. These different roles and involvements caused some difficulties. As employees, we had more time working in the ecovillage and, thus, more influence in decisions that were made.
- Deciding the makeup of the Board: In the beginning, everyone in the ecovillage could be a member of the Board. While this was very inclusive, it was also unpredictable because anyone could show up at a meeting anytime and still be a decision maker. Plus, there were many different ideas for what people wanted to see happen.
- Dealing with conflicts: Like all organizations, we experienced some conflicts about how things or monies should proceed or be processed. We strive to be as transparent as possible, though personality conflicts are inevitable.

In terms of making decisions, Deborah feels the Board has made strides to be more organized and accountable. Although not everyone on the Board is always well-versed in consensus, it is written into the bylaws. One of the critical factors in working together is trust and respect. The Board's informal structure can help build relationships, so it can work better, and members can make decisions together. Having good meeting processes and a clear agenda, with proposals from committees, improves meetings. Good processes help make good decisions. Sometimes processes get tedious though. Deborah remembers when one committee proposed a mural on the ecovillage's apartment building (Burr Oak Building or BOB) wall to increase the visibility of the ecovillage. The committee did the research and had a plan, but the Board did not agree with the proposal. One person suggested a community design process that was started, but never finished. BOB is still bare.

There are many things Deborah appreciates about the ecovillage:

- Being able to share in this experiment
- Living in a diverse neighborhood
- Trading and borrowing with neighbors
- Sharing contagious do-it-yourself projects like setting up rooftop water catchment and trying to get "off the grid"
- Growing gardens and food
- Taking her dog on a walk and meeting up with others for a chat
- Participating in activities and potlucks
- Walking in the woods around the ridge

She also thinks there is always more that could be developed, such as a healing center, elder care, a shared car, and more organized reflection about how we're doing.

Deborah feels that people in the ecovillage are trying to live shared values together and, being human, doing it in imperfect ways. She feels that good group process is needed to help do that. Decision-making is an art that can be practiced. She likes this quote: "Decisions made today determine how tomorrow will be."

CHAPTER 5

The Excitement and Tensions of Creating Intimacy and Close Friendships

Several years ago, as I leaned back on an oak tree in a quiet area of the two-hundred acres of woods that surround our ecovillage, it became clear that I was not alone. I had come to the woods because I was nervous about planning our first EarthSpirit Rising Conference for 400 people. The tree I sat under and the surrounding ecosystem held a wisdom I was able to share. It became very clear that the conference was going to work. I never worried about it again, and it did work out. This type of experience I have had at other times among the trees of forested areas, though this was the first time it had come to me so close to home. I stopped and began to listen. I felt a non-judgmental, wise, and open presence.

It is a message so gentle, yet so frightening for a scientifically educated westerner, that I still have occasion to doubt its legitimacy. But, when I am courageous enough, I can accept that I am an interdependent, totally interrelated part of this mystical, magical Earth. When I am in this place, I experience the greatest of intimacy with the natural world, which includes the human species, animals, and the plants and trees. It is within this gentle array of intimacy that the ecovillage began.

What Intimacy Looks Like

Intimacy is a key part of any ecovillage. I define intimacy as willful, conscious interdependence. Because we have a culture that encourages us to meet our needs in diverse places, usually outside our neighborhood, we do not need to be interdependent with our neighbors, with people in our work setting, church, school, or in any of the many places we spend time with others. For some people it is possible to develop meaningful relationships outside of the intimacy of one's neighborhood. For example, my sister fell in love with her future husband through letters and telephone calls. Likewise, in our urban ecovillage we encourage our residents to have friendships and relationships in the larger sphere of the city, state, or world, though we also put more emphasis on choosing to be interdependent with each other in our ecovillage.

Intimacy often begins within the family—husband, wife and possibly children. The question is, how do we move beyond this? There are many ways.

In our own home, Eileen and I have had other people living with us through most of our married life. Over the years we have used the third story of our home to rent out to family and friends. We share our meals and common rooms with them. This has expanded the intimacy within our own household. It has also had an effect on our children's ability to relate well with others.

Moving beyond the family, being close by to others in the same neighborhood, makes it easier to connect on a frequent basis.

This, too, opens up the possibility for intimacy. And, of course, having the *same reason* as a neighbor for living in the neighborhood makes intimacy an even greater possibility; our ecovillage shares our connection with Earth. Our conversations and our interactions in Earth-related events enhance connections and intimacy.

Most of us in the ecovillage also take great joy in feeling intimacy with the land and other species that live close by. Feeding the birds and squirrels, caring for trees and other plants, and being open to listening to them is another level of intimacy and friendship. During a serious drought, I ran three hundred feet of hose going back into the woods to water the oak tree I spend a lot of time with. I felt it was the least I could do.

Challenges

Part of the reality we deal with in converting an existing neighborhood into an ecovillage is that we do not have a lot to say about who moves in. We do not have the power to interview and accept or reject residents. When a home is listed for sale, it does so on the open market. We do reach out to see if we can find someone to purchase the home who is interested in the Earth and in being part of our ecovillage. And most of the time the person who moves here has this interest, but not always. Even then, there is no way to assess whether they will fit in well in the ecovillage, or if we are a good fit for them. Therefore, there are no obligations or expectations of those who move here, just a hope and invitation for them to be an active part of this way of life.

We have a half dozen households move to the ecovillage each year, some renting, and some buying. When someone new moves here, we have a tradition of going to meet them, offering them food, a meal, and a welcome to the ecovillage. Often, the people who move here come because of the ecovillage but without knowing anyone. It would be easy to let them fall through the cracks. It is especially easy since there are a number of "old timers" who know each other well, and they have formed relationships that could seem exclusive to a new person if no one were to reach out to them. We often introduce new folks in the monthly newsletter and have a small blurb about them. We make a special effort to invite them to events that take place in the ecovillage: potluck dinners, front porch gatherings, and pancake breakfasts where everyone in the ecovillage and the neighborhood is invited. Having started to charge a $15 membership fee, we also give them a year free membership to the ecovillage. This is the beginning of relationship building—or not—because no one is required to be involved. It is merely an opportunity.

A second struggle we encounter is that, for most people who move here, the ecovillage is an add-on. Most of them already live in the Cincinnati area. They are established, have a job, a church, and friendships. A few people have moved here from other cities to start over, but the majority of people moving here are from Cincinnati. Whereas an ecovillage begun from scratch is generally located in a rural area, it requires almost all residents to relocate from somewhere afar and leaves them few options but to start a new life, usually with the ecovillage as a main focus of their daily chores and activities. This is not generally true in the urban ecovillage that starts within an existing neighborhood.

As such, some people take the opportunities available and run with them by becoming a core part of the ecovillage experience and developing a real sense of intimacy with other residents, while others do not. We have people who seem to be a perfect fit for the ecovillage but end up almost isolated from the experience. Others make a real effort to become part of what is happening, and they succeed. One person moved into an ecovillage-rehabbed home, joined the communications committee, and after only a year was elected the chairperson of the ecovillage Board. While she's a quiet person, she holds an obvious excitement to be part of our community. Another person moved here from a distant city and quickly joined the Board and has been a key player. One person moved here from another city, became extremely active with the housing committee, and moved it to a level of real importance, only to divorce and move away.

While there are real stresses to intimacy in the urban retrofit ecovillage, as in most villages and communities, there are people who develop strong relationships. There are couples, families, and singles who form more intimate relationships with each other. While there are no publicly known polyamorous relationships in the community, intimate friendships develop that are supportive and intellectually stimulating. Sometimes these relationships can be challenging when intimate relationships disintegrate, such as in divorces.

Ways of Coming Together

There are both structured and unstructured ways people are drawn together. As in most communities, children and animals draw people together. Specifically, children bring families together. This happens in many settings but seems to have a special influence in developing intimate relationships in the ecovillage. There are houses where parents love to have children gather and play together, often in some type of ecological focus. This not only helps with the relationships among the children but also among the parents, who have an opportunity to engage with each other while the children play and to teach like-minded values about the Earth to their kids.

People stop to talk to others who have children with them as well as people who are walking their dogs. We have had a dog-walking group who meet every Sunday at the Imago Earth Center to let their dogs run and give the people a chance to relate. Others walk their dogs together every day. This is very similar to other neighborhoods where families relate well with each other. The difference is in the support given to each other to care deeply for Earth and to share this with the children.

Our urban CSA, which is dispersed among various plots in ten backyards in the ecovillage, is also a way people communicate and relate to other people, plants, animals, and soils. The farmers among us use this setting to share a deep connection with the elements of the earth. The CSA has also proven to be a great catalyst for people to get to know and care for each other, and through their work requirement, they're taught a deep appreciation, affection, and a realization of their interdependence with the plants and soil they work with.

While there are many challenges to intimacy, the urban ecovillage provides a great deal to residents who live here. The membership committee has a focus of bringing people together through quarterly meetings, giving them opportunities to bond and work together. Intimacy is one of the real positives and will remain a constant issue for the urban ecovillage to expand around. Figuring this out will continue to be challenging and exciting.

These Enchanting Woods

This is also true in our relationships with other species. While I sat under the large oak tree in the woods surrounding the eco-village, a huge murder of crows was forming and loudly expressing its presence. The crow is a sign of mystery and magic. They remind me that we are part of this amazing Earth. While sitting inside our houses, looking at our flat-screened computers and televisions or reading words in books, it is so easy to forget that we are part of this incredible, mysterious planet. However, it is by being present to this larger community of other species, of water, soil, and clouds that we can find the intimacy that truly connects all of us. This connection and appreciation of Earth is the underlying connection of intimacy within our ecovillage. But it is the human connections, supporting each other to see the ecovillage as more than human, that makes it possible to defy the beliefs of this culture and become intimate with the human and non-human world surrounding us.

Intimacy: Ken Reidel

Ken has always gardened. His parents grew flowers, vegetables, and fruit trees. As a child, he loved to pick and eat fruit right off the tree. In college, he was a fine-arts major. He worked for the Cincinnati Recreation Department for fifteen years, starting as a lifeguard and advancing to an administrative position. One day he went to volunteer at the Miami Township Senior Center in Cleves, Ohio (a suburb of Cincinnati), and before the day was out, they asked him to apply for the job as director. He accepted the job, and earned $5,000 less per year, but he enjoyed the position and being his own boss. While he was the director, he and his family lived on a farm in Indiana, where they had twelve acres with a large garden, goats, and chickens. He drove fifty miles one-way each day to get to work. It was an hour drive, but it was through a scenic area, and he used the time to plan his day as he drove in and reflected on his day on the way home. He quit at age sixty-two, after twenty-eight years at the senior center.

As he was planning to retire, he began thinking about where he would like to live. After he separated from his wife and his children left home, he moved to Cincinnati and loved his urban home. When his son Nate moved to the ecovillage, Ken came to some events. He decided he wanted to live in a community and not just a neighborhood. The ecovillage gave him the added incentive of living close to his son and grandchildren. He looked for a house to purchase in the ecovillage for two years because he wanted a place that backed into the 200-acre woods and where he could have a large garden. When the house next door to his son went on the market, it had everything he wanted plus his family next door. He bought it and has lived there for nine years.

The focus on ecology and on living in harmony with our planet and universe was another reason he was drawn to the ecovillage. He experienced a degree of environmental awareness in workshops and seasonal celebrations. With this support he has tried to leave the smallest footprint and do his part to ensure for future generations a world that educates, protects, and respects our planet.

The ecovillage has proven to be everything he wanted and more. He loves the following:

- The opportunity to learn and volunteer with other people in the ecovillage
- The fact that many young families have moved here, and more buildings are available for new families
- That everyone watches out for the children
- The camaraderie of sitting on his front porch and talking to people. He has gotten to know almost everyone

He has found the ecovillage to be a great place for intimacy on so many levels. For Ken, intimacy is watching each other's back and also turning to each other for advice or anything that is needed. Part of it is the great amount of sharing that goes on. If a person needs a tool or help, someone is always there to offer a hand. For his part, Ken loves being around children and finds it a wonderful opportunity to watch other people's kids for a little while if parents need to get something done or need a break.

Since Nate lives next door to his dad, he is able to enjoy the greater intimacy of family. He discusses with him ways of raising his children, how to share their garden space, and they are available to each other in times of crisis or support through illness. The children get the opportunity to be deeply cared about by their grandfather on a daily basis.

Ken feels lucky to be retired. Although he works a lot harder than when he had a job, a good part of it is being able to give to others in the ecovillage. He is now able to give a lot more than he receives in his retirement, but someday he knows it will come back and equal out. At this time in his life, Ken likes that he can pick and choose what he wants to do. He loves working with the CSA, at the greenhouse, and at the ecovillage pub. These are all things that help bring residents of the ecovillage together. He is pleased that the ecovillage is expanding to new streets, which will allow more like-minded families to be part of it.

He is also very happy with the improved communication in the ecovillage, such as using the email listserve, which allows anyone to see the minutes of meetings and know what is happening. Since he hates meetings but likes to know what is going on with the people around him, this is ideal for him and an important part of intimacy. It lays the groundwork for reaching out and communicating directly with people.

Ken feels that he has found his place and revels every day in the intimate relationships that have developed for him in the ecovillage. He looks forward to forming other close relationships in the future.

CHAPTER 6

Conflict

Part One: Transitioning in the Ecovillage—A Rocky Time by Jim Schenk

We began the Enright Ridge Urban Ecovillage in 2004, and because Imago was the parent organization, I became the project coordinator. The Ecovillage originally set up a Board of Directors for the organization which consisted of residents of the community who chose to be members. We began a big project of purchasing and rehabbing foreclosed properties in the ecovillage—something that I had both the resources and experience to do.

The original group proceeded to develop the Board, select officers, and set up committees. The Board and committees did an incredible amount of work in the areas of housing, beautification, marketing, conservation, and the recruiting of new members. They also assigned me the title of Ecovillage Coordinator and paid me a salary of $100 per week through Imago. The pay was not much, but it did designate me as paid staff, which helped in relating to other organizations and funders.

Residents of the ecovillage carried out much of the work. However, I had a great deal of influence in determining the direction because of time spent, years of experience in community organizing and administration, commitment to developing an ecovillage, and my position. I had a central role in the buying and the rehab planning of houses the ecovillage bought. I helped develop a budget and raised funds to hire additional staff. I gave many presentations about the ecovillage and was responsible for bringing in many new members and volunteers.

In the fall of 2008, we acknowledged that the organization needed to delegate more leadership, and we began talking about developing stronger committees that would take on more responsibility. Toward this end we planned the Board meeting in January 2009 using a "storyboard" system. At this meeting we told the story of each committee, putting the information on cards and placing them on a pegboard with stickpins. This gave the ecovillage Board a chance to see what each committee was doing. The meeting was a great success.

For the next meeting we planned to look at the storyboard to find overlaps and areas not being covered. All the committees were excited to meet and map out their projects and goals for 2009. By the end of the month, we had documents from everyone, and it seemed like a positive transition would naturally progress.

However, at the February meeting, the process met unexpected challenges. One member began the meeting by accusing the Housing Committee of doing shoddy work and not handling the funds for the houses well. This was followed by another member demanding that we hand out a list of all income and expenses for all the houses at each Board meeting. A third member, who had a dislike for me, chimed in her support. The treasurer of the ecovillage expressed her confidence in the bookkeeping, which did little to squelch the demands.

I knew that giving people a 40-page itemized list of income and expenses each month was not the way to help them make sense of finances. However, I told them I would be willing to sit down with anyone and go over our books. Then I would be willing to run off any information still desired. No one accepted the offer, and the demands to run off the numerous pages of financial information continued. I refused. The meeting ended in turmoil and a power struggle began.

I believed it would blow over—it did not. Accusations continued and I could feel the beginning of sides forming. Several months passed without any resolution.

We agreed to bring in a mediator to help with the conflict. The session was scheduled for July. Two days before the session I received word that my brother in Venezuela had died. My priority became to attend his funeral. However, the group decided to still hold the mediation session with my consent.

When I returned, I was told that the mediation session had occurred, and that the mediator was summarizing the session. It had been decided that we should have another session with the mediator, this time with me present. I was handed the mediator's report at a session held the following month. Much of it was negatively directed at me, most of it around finances, with some general statements of appreciation for starting the ecovillage. During this meeting, some people criticized the report because a lot more positive things were said about me at the July session than recorded in the document. The majority of the 15 people at the meeting were silent in this regard. Not having had time to really digest the material, I had little to say except to ask some clarifying questions. I was personally hurt by the silence.

I mulled over this report for several days. Finally, at the end of July, I wrote a somewhat scathing response. Since finances continued to be the main issue, I offered to set up a time to sit down with any members to go over the books with them and provide them with printed information of anything they wanted at that time. I offered to hand over the financial books to anyone who wanted to take them on. I also told them that since they were paying me $100 per week, and the going rate of someone with my experience would be a minimum of $50 per hour, I was willing to do whatever they wanted me to do for two hours per week. The rest of my time I would volunteer, doing what I felt was appropriate like everyone else. However, if they wanted me to continue as coordinator, I needed three things:

1. Have this document rewritten so that it reflects the positive contributions I have made to the ecovillage that at least equals the length of the negative statements,
2. Include the strengths and weaknesses of those attending the mediation sessions and the changes they need to make.
3. Reflect the incredible accomplishments we have made together in only six years.

Two people responded by writing what they saw as my positive contributions, but the Board president told me that the mediator's report was a final document and could not be altered. This made it clear to me that the beautiful opportunity for shared power that opened up in January was now dead in the water.

Despite all that happened, I continued most of the work that I had been doing before because I was (and am) deeply committed to the idea and the organization. In fact, 2009 was a very successful year for the ecovillage. The Urban Community Supported Agriculture project was a huge success. I wrote a proposal that was funded to hire two AmeriCorps Volunteers. We wrote a grant and received money to pay off the Greenhouse for the CSA. We completed the rehab of two houses. In addition, a number of new people moved into the ecovillage.

However, no one else stepped forward to take over any of my responsibilities nor did anyone want to go over the finances, until, after some cajoling, I was finally able to get four people, one being the treasurer, to review the books with me. This was done just before the September Board meeting. Their report stated that the books were in good shape.

Because no one stepped forward to take over any of my responsibilities for $100 per week, I also recommended the following to the Board:

1. Consider how much it would cost to hire someone for the coordinator. If the Board still wants me to volunteer my time to the degree in which I had been working for the ecovillage, it needs to figure out a way to compensate me.
2. Consider someone else in the ecovillage to be the volunteer Or decide to run without one.

On the first of October 2009, only my request to have members look at the books had been met and the Board had not followed any of my recommendations. At this time, I felt it necessary, both for my own sanity and for the ecovillage, that I resign as coordinator. I did this by writing a letter to the president of the Board on October 11. I offered to stay on as long as the Board wanted me, but no longer than December 31. Within four days, I had a letter from the president saying that they accepted my resignation. It was clear to me that I had made the right decision.

The Board approached me to understand the many facets of my role. I typed out a three-page list of my responsibilities and tasks and offered them to the five people who met with me. I explained each of the items as best I could and offered to consult with them during the transition. The next three months were somewhat unnerving because very little movement was happening around the upcoming transition. The Board instead concentrated on developing a new mission statement and bylaws.

January 1st came, and barely any transition had taken place. The Board was not scheduled to hold their first meeting until the end of January. I had offered to do a few things like supervise staff since I was the only one authorized by AmeriCorps. The Board rejected this offer even though they had worked out no means of supervising them. Finally, at the end of January, the transition of responsibilities and tasks began.

I refused to allow myself to become vindictive during this process. I won't say that it did not hurt, but I understand power, leadership, and transitioning. Understanding did not totally take away the feeling of rejection and the lack of appreciation. But despite these feelings, I was determined to be available to help in the transition because the ecovillage was (and is) very important to me.

One of my strengths is being able to give up power. This I have done a number of times at different organizations and groups. However, I did catch myself automatically doing some of my previous jobs. For example, soon after the transition, it snowed twelve inches, and the houses we rehabbed were still empty. One of my fears is having the ecovillage houses look vacant, which makes them a mark for being broken into. I began shoveling the snow at one of these vacant properties. My wife pointed out that I was no longer on the Housing Committee and so this was neither my responsibility nor my right anymore. With great reluctance, I quit.

The disruptions of 2009 with the loss of staff and the development of a new structure led to struggles on the Board during 2010. What resulted was a period in which there were only five Board members, after the president and many of the other members resigned. The Board itself became immobilized. The question arose whether the nonprofit organization should continue. While the Board accomplished very little that year, a decision to disband was not made. Some of the committees continued to function well during this year, others not so well.

With 2011 came a new group of Board members who were committed to working together. The conflicts receded, and the Board functioned as intended, with most of its committees operating well.

Through all of this, the Communications, Ecovillage Green Group, and CSA Committees continued to carry out their tasks. The Housing Committee deteriorated to a one-person responsibility that led to some major inefficiencies, and a decrease in income from housing, which was one of the major sources of operating funds for the ecovillage.

The year 2012 began with a retreat of the Board, a manual for Board members, and a real effort to solidify the positive actions of 2011. As a result, the ecovillage has continued, new people have moved here, and new leadership became involved. That time of crisis has passed, and opportunity evolved.

It frequently takes stick-to-itiveness to get through a period like this. Despite the conflict, I have stayed engaged because I believe this community is worth fighting for and the urban ecovillage is worth developing as a model for how we can live sustainably in our cities. Enright Ridge Urban Ecovillage continues as an organization because enough people felt it was a worthwhile undertaking and were willing to take on a difficult situation and make it work again.

Part Two: Conflict Happens by Deborah Jordan

I wish we all would write up our versions of what happened and share them. Maybe we could understand each other better and take responsibility for our part in the conflict. Having worked in visionary nonprofits for twenty years, I know expectations can be high without the necessary skills to totally fulfill them, and disappointments can ensue.

Jim (and Eileen) have initiated some amazing projects and organizations where I have tried to be a worker bee. Some people used the term "founder's syndrome" to describe our ecovillage conflict; they did not want Jim leading the way anymore. Founder's syndrome means the organizational structure can take on the strengths and weaknesses of the founder, plus he/she needs to know when it is time to move on. Since the founder (Jim) lives on the street, he was involved with the transition of power. Why then did the ecovillage temporarily turn into a soap opera?

Some of the key dilemmas I heard voiced: are we building a non-profit, a community, or an eco-community? Are we doing everything right? Do I know everything going on?

I was content with what we were doing, but some others were not. People moved to the ecovillage for what they perceived was happening, but there was no application or discernment process for membership and no orientation. We had dual roles as neighbors, ecovillage members, and some as employees. Plus, we had other aspects of our lives, such as jobs, away from Enright. We were "creating the road (to an ecovillage) as we walked." Instead of dealing with key dilemmas, too often, we had "parking lot" conversations instead of whole group conversations. We had several members who were so frustrated they used e-mail and a meeting or two to blame and attack, which fueled people taking sides. We had no clear conflict resolution processes. My attempted mediation in one of the conflicts failed because I was perceived as Jim's supporter. Some of us did not know each other well enough to have trust or commitment to continue to take the increased time to work things out.

Yes, conflict happens, even in ecovillages. In fact, it is one reason many people never get beyond envisioning an ecovillage community. As we know, conflict can be productive, but it can also be destructive if not handled well. Anyone who has lived with others knows that our needs, wants, and values can collide on a daily basis. Then what happens when we mix a lot more people and cultures together in a neighborhood where not everyone has signed onto the ecovillage concept? Add in some uncomfortable feelings or some self-righteous attitudes, and there will be clashes or avoidance.

Conflict is complex. A number of ecovillage residents shared the following (**in bold**) about the subject of conflict:

- **Interpersonal conflict is common.** So true, and how we handle it is important.
- **Conflict is inevitable.** The willingness to offer a conscious effort at resolution is as good a deed as an organizing an event for the ecovillage. Good deeds build metaphorical bridges.
- **There is more impetus to resolve conflict with family and friends.** There are different levels of relations in the ecovillage. People may not feel the need to resolve conflict with neighbors as much as with family and friends. When do neighbors become friends?
- **Trying to adopt policies to deal with conflict can sometimes be reactionary.** "Wet blanket" policies can cover too much territory and dampen both positive and negative efforts.
- **Do not let your ego get in the way.** Ego reacts and defends and gets in the way of understanding.
- **It is not always personal.** Even if ego insists it is.
- **Communication can be at the root of conflict.** It is hard to slow down and listen when someone knows they're right. Okay, maybe they just think they are.
- **Seeking first to understand helps.** Sounds like the golden rule
- **Different projects and activities have different inner and outer circles.** Being part of the inner circle means more input but also more work. Maybe we all do not need to know everything.
- **Useful group conflict processes often involve cooperative styles.** We need to learn and practice and encode cooperative

processes to resolve conflict, using processes such as negotiation or mediation.

Conflict resolution involves people, issues, and processes. People have egos, personalities, and feelings. One reason many want to avoid conflict is that it feels uncomfortable, or even painful. We care about what others think of us. It is often scary to conflict with people because there is a possibility that, while we are working to resolve an issue, animosity could be the result.

Some of the Issues

Then there are the issues. The ecovillage board has to decide whether to buy a house or how to deal with a budget shortfall. People have different opinions. Sometimes the external issue seems small, such as what to name a committee, but the external issue is the focal point for internal values or needs. We are disagreeing about who should have a say, who is right, and ultimately about our visions for the future.

Not surprisingly, some common hot-button issues are financial. We receive income from rentals but need to pay back our housing loans. Ongoing conflicts have occurred related to housing since it is one of the bigger projects and one of the bigger risks, and it involves money. Housing rehabs have helped stabilize the neighborhood, but they're big, risky projects. People have different ways of approaching rehabs. If you've ever tried to decide about the color of a room with a group of people, multiply that difficulty many times over. We have done remarkably well with these challenging issues. Historically, one of the biggest conflict issues was related to leadership and housing, and of course, money was connected to housing. Lines were drawn, righteousness mounted, a mediator was employed, and time was needed to help heal rifts.

Approaching Conflict

People have also learned different styles of approaching conflict that relate to the processes used in dealing with it. Under stress, we often revert to patterns of fight or flight. These styles can be made more memorable by referencing animals: lion (aggressive), turtle (avoid), chameleon (accommodate), zebra (compromise), and dolphin (collaborate). Each style has its positives and negatives and can be useful. Dolphins and zebras are helpful in meetings. Lions can get things done. Not all conflict has to be or can be resolved. Sometimes we move on thanks to chameleons and turtles.

While conflict comes in many forms, how conflict is presented can be an important part of framing the problem or fanning the fire. Instead of blaming, naming the conflict in ways all parties can agree on is helpful. What did not work in our ecovillage is that people made personal attacks, ignored critiques, and took the conflict to our e-mail listserve. Emotions escalated. We have had people blow up at meetings or walk out, and some people have quit. These reactions have ripple effects.

It is hard to talk about conflict without talking about community contexts. People move here for many reasons: like-minded people, affordability, proximity to downtown, surrounding woods, and to be part of demonstrating the urban ecovillage concept. The ecovillage has inherited and developed many wonderful assets and opportunities, such as the Imago Earth Center, Terry Street Commons (a small outdoor gathering place for bonfires and such), CSA and greenhouse, food-buying club, potlucks, Zen Center (a spiritual center located in the ecovillage but privately owned), and housing rehabs. It is an exciting urban neighborhood. There is definitely fluidity as some move here, then move on, especially from rentals. There is also a stable core of people.

People choose to get involved for many reasons. The mission statement is "Enright Ridge Urban Ecovillage seeks to be an ecologically responsible community sharing ideas, resources, and a reverence for the Earth." ERUEV is interesting and loosely structured. There is no screening process for joining or enjoying many of our assets. People can buy or rent a place and become informal members just by showing up. By paying a small fee, they can become members. This lack of boundaries is welcoming and inclusive. Sometimes, however, it is frustrating because it can lead to conflict. The mission draws like-minded people in the broad sense, but particular interests may vary. For instance, some may be more interested in community, and others in homesteading.

There is, as yet, no formal orientation to the ecovillage so it helps if newcomers take their own initiative to get involved or know someone who can be a bridge to the community.

While we hope people who move here will get involved, they sometimes do not, but can still be good neighbors. Some people prefer the formal structure, while some prefer informality. Probably the formal structures have generated more known conflict between residents except for next-door neighbor issues like wrangling over on-street parking.

Rubbing Each Other the Wrong Way

Even if there are no philosophical differences, we can also "rub each other the wrong way." Not only is it a challenge to live in community; we have more to learn about how to deal with differences in community. Community can be considered "rubbing each other into shape." We have passionate people who choose to live here and want support. Many of us have been on the edge of mainstream beliefs so when we move here, we're willing to stand up for our views. Perhaps this makes it harder to compromise. And, of course, ideals do not match reality.

How can we remember that conflict is a growth opportunity? Third parties, living either inside or outside the ecovillage, can help fuel or tame the conflict. Sometimes we share our concerns with others who are not involved. Spreading rumors can cause conflicts whereas sharing with a neutral third party can encourage understanding about what happened. A neighbor started making negative comments to and about another resident, who became agitated. Others verified that the neighbor had health problems, and this helped increase understanding, so cooler heads prevailed.

Working It Out

It is easy to focus on the negatives with conflict but there have been a number of positives as we work through issues. It is refreshing to know we can reconcile even if we disagree. Taking a break can help. People can come in and out of the formal and informal structures. Walking in the neighborhood is good for the usual health reasons but also for interacting with others in a nonthreatening way. Reaching out can help reconciliation. One resident apologized for his behavior by taking another to breakfast and sharing his struggles. Coming together in rituals or potlucks or beer brewing can also help. We share lots of potlucks where we can normalize relations by talking about food or the environment or children or the season.

Many people have spiritual practices that are sometimes shared, such as in our organized Earth-centered rituals. These spiritual practices can allow us to get to know each other in a deeper way. Understanding the life challenges we all deal with can help grow empathy and compassion. In the past, friends in the neighborhood used the Enneagram, a Sufi personality system, to help understand each other's personality differences.

Finally, people do have other aspects of their lives. Living in the ecovillage is just one dimension. If this dimension gets too intense, people can take a break. Whether it is having young children and/ or a job in or outside the neighborhood, people are busy. As we continue to share our lives and interests, we will have joys, struggles and conflict. This is part of living in an ecovillage.

With all that, we continue to be an imperfect model of creating an urban ecovillage in an existing transitional neighborhood. We are trying to be bridge builders. I'm trying to learn my boundaries and take on what I enjoy. This means I step back at times and let others do the sometimes-unappreciated organizational work. That's true in general with many people moving in and out of leadership here. It is also helpful to remember that people will often step up when asked to contribute, including me; I am a good worker bee when asked. What a relief that people have not taken any new conflicts to e-mail. We still have a lot to learn about transparent decision making and nonviolent communication, although we do now have a conflict resolution "policy." Finally, the vision is so important. We are urban pioneers where amazing projects abound. May we all learn and grow together in service to the planet and each other.

CHAPTER 7

Acquiring Resources

Because we began the ecovillage in an existing neighborhood, the day we met, the ecovillage could begin. To start a "retrofit" ecovillage, it takes only three or four households in close proximity to join together to make it happen. If people want to join, they only need to rent or buy. Purchasing an existing home can take a month or two, instead of years as is probable in a rural ecovillage.

With a retrofit ecovillage many of the resources are already in place to make up its foundation. Enright Ridge Urban Ecovillage began with many of its needed resources: houses, people's skills with creativity, natural resources in the form of land, animals, and plants, as well as finances. And much of this was available the day we began.

Housing

People do not need a lot of money to find housing in our eco-village. Rentals, purchases, and rehabs do not require a lot of funds in this inner-ring neighborhood, one that is close to downtown. We have houses as inexpensive as $12,000 up to $120,000, with most of them in the $50,000 to $75,000 range.

People—Skills, Collective Resources and Creativity

Many of the needs we have are carried out by the people who live here. Our brochure, newsletter, and flyers have been created by graphic designers who live in the village. Articles for our ecovillage monthly newsletter are e-mailed to the newsletter coordinator, put together in one document, and sent to another person who lays it out each month. Our only expense is printing the newsletter.

Many of the tasks of the ecovillage are carried out by volunteers. People are available to share their knowledge about carpentry or give the name of a carpenter who could help out if they can't. This is also true of plumbing and plumbers, cleaning, and green cleaners. Cooking, canning, and knowledge about harvesting plants and animals are shared. I have taught a number of people in the ecovillage how to can their food. Those who have hens share their knowledge with new owners. We can put out requests for tools, transportation, or "a cup of sugar" via our ecovillage listserv. For example, a number of people share a log-splitter. We also share in labor. We have had people helping with the houses we have renovated doing demolition, painting, or cleaning. It is an endless list of resources that we exchange and share.

Since many people have lived here for a while, there is a large supply of tools and equipment shared, along with a great deal of knowledge and wisdom. Basic carpentry tools can be borrowed, or a resident who owns the tools will help others by using their tools and skills. For example, a person who owns a Bobcat is willing to help a neighbor by digging a trench or removing a tree stump. We have grinders, paint equipment, garden tools, vehicles, computers, and the list goes on of things available for people to borrow. In the future we are hoping for a formalized tool exchange system, but this is not available yet.

People from the ecovillage are also hired by neighbors to carry out major tasks in their skill sets. One person has insulated some twenty-five houses in the ecovillage. We have people providing childcare. There are electricians, carpenters, lawyers, graphic designers, mediators, among other professions. This works well because ecovillagers are hiring people they know and because the person doing the work reduces the amount of travel. In most cases people give a discount to neighbors and community members.

As a way to accomplish projects, we have collectively raised funds to purchase land that we preserved in the ecovillage. When an attempt was made to build new housing on a green space at the end of Enright Avenue, the community came together to stop this development. Then we raised $27,000 to acquire 3 1/2 acres in order to keep it as green space.

In some cases, we have come up with creative solutions to help each other out. For example, one person who was very involved in the ecovillage needed to purchase a work truck, so he asked several people if they would provide him with the funds he needed to purchase it in exchange for his working for them in the future. The neighborhood devised a method they called Billybucks, (Billy was his name) which provided him with funds in exchange for his rehab and carpentry skills. With the Billybucks, some money he had saved, and a donation, Billy was able to purchase a dependable truck.

We are an ecovillage where the majority of people are financially stable. If there is a strong need for funds, either to support the ecovillage itself, or to help someone in the community, there are dependable resources. There are also people who understand financial and legal systems who can help both the ecovillage and individuals meet their needs. One family was losing their home to foreclosure, and a neighbor was able to purchase it. Since the family was not interested in buying the house back due to huge medical debts, they have been able to rent the house and remain in their home of forty years. Another individual who was having a hard time finding work was hired to help work on some of the houses in the ecovillage, providing him with funds needed to pay rent and meet his needs.

Not All Resources Are Financial

One of our resources is our informal united efforts to help individuals, families, or the organization when they are under stress. Many people know each other well enough to help out if a friend or neighbor is struggling in any way. It is often a comfort for members to know that food will be brought over, or gardens will be tended if one is sick, out of town, or needing emotional support. However, one of the weaknesses of a retrofit ecovillage where the majority of people are not members is that some people tend to live a more private life and do not share if they are having troubles.

The ecovillage encourages people joining together and supporting each other in reaching their personal goals. For example, Megan Divelbiss and a friend linked together in learning to become Waldorf educators. They traveled together to the training in Chicago and worked together at a Waldorf School nearby. They were a support system for each other. Megan has since opened her own preschool Waldorf center in the ecovillage.

Others, knowing the interest of individuals living here, have been able to make contacts that have helped them find work that is meaningful, from helping contractors find work to helping people find a job. For example, when Dan Divelbiss wanted to start his own plant-growing business, a resident pointed out an available funding source. He was able to start a very successful business.

Natural Resources

I always hesitate to put land, animals, and plants in the resource category because this tends to objectify them, but they are an essential part of our community. Even though we are only seven minutes from downtown Cincinnati, we have 200+ acres of woods and green space surrounding our dead-end streets. The ecovillage did not acquire this resource, it was already here as part of our community. Most people's homes are on lots ranging from a quarter-acre to five acres. This land is connected to what's called the Western Wildlife Corridor that runs some twenty miles along the Ohio River to the Great Miami River, close to the Indiana border. As a result, we have numerous deer, raccoons, a full array of birds, sometimes foxes, and even an occasional mountain lion.

We have developed a two-mile walking trail through the woods surrounding the ecovillage. With the advice of a resident lawyer, we wrote to people to let them know that we wanted to build a walking trail through the woods and would be going through their land. We asked them to let us know if they had any objections. Only one person had an issue; he owned a property but lived out-of-state. He eventually sold it to Imago, and so we were able to create a lovely path for everyone on Enright Avenue, not just ecovillage members.

Imago has been able to acquire close to forty acres of land surrounding the ecovillage. Sixteen acres are part of the Imago Earth Center, where Imago's offices are located and where it offers programs for both children and adults. Another twenty-four acres are accessed from the end of Enright Avenue. Some of the acreage will be used as a garden for the CSA. While using some of the land for program purposes, the primary motivation for acquiring the acreage was to provide habitat for other species.

We have also been creative in our use of available natural resources. When we started the urban CSA, we needed additional land. We approached ecovillage residents about using their back-yards for garden space. Many of them lent their land and signed an agreement within two months. Eileen and I offered our garden of 35 years for the CSA to use. These days, the CSA is made up primarily of backyards and lots that are "owned" by individuals, the ecovillage, or Imago. Everyone who lends land is offered some benefit toward their CSA membership, though only a few people actually accept it.

Financial Resources

Many ecovillage residents work outside the neighborhood. Be-cause people live simply, they can do the things they love, such as being AmeriCorps volunteer, work part time, start their own busi-ness, or work at home. People frequently move here from within the city, and thus often arrive already employed. We have five people working at the public library, four others are Waldorf teachers. We also have social workers, pharmacists, lawyers, maintenance workers, auto mechanics, entrepreneurs, and the list goes on.

Several of us are attempting to see how close we can come to living off the grid. Photovoltaic cells, solar hot water, cisterns, wood-burning stoves, well-insulated homes—these are all steps that some people are taking. Frequently this is done through private income. People also use other sources of funds. Some are borrowed, but there are also grants, tax deductions, and rebates that can help make one's home more energy efficient.

The two largest expenses for the ecovillage come from the houses we purchase to sell or rent and from the CSA project. Both the houses and the CSA generate income to cover their expenses. Hous-ing, in most years, has produced an income over expenses, which provided revenue for ecovillage programs. Maintaining an income of $20,000 per year the first five years and $10,000 per year since then has been very manageable. This is not to say there were not times when some belt tightening was necessary. However, compared to the cost of starting an ecovillage from the ground up, the financial issues have been minor.

In 2012, the ecovillage's total expenses, aside from houses and the CSA, were under $10,000. This included $3600 we paid Imago for the use of the Imago Earth Center for meetings, office space, a bookkeeping system, and telephone usage. In addition, we pay for our bookkeeper, taxes, and insurance for the houses and properties we own, along with memberships in other organizations. These are all minor expenses compared to the cost of purchasing land, building houses, developing the infrastructure and so much more when starting from scratch as in rural ecovillages.

When Imago needed to raise $27,000 to purchase a beautiful meadow and wooded area in the ecovillage, we asked residents and friends to donate. This brought in the funds needed. In my over 40+ years of working for ecological causes, I've noticed that people tend to want to donate money to preserve land. I believe there may be an innate awareness of our deep connection with land.

Other sources of income have included funds from the houses we rehab and sell, from charging for tours of the ecovillage, membership fees, sustainers (people in or interested in the ecovillage who commit to contributing $500 per year or more for five years), workshops, presentations, and fundraisers.

As a nonprofit organization we have been able to apply and receive grants for the work we are doing. For example, we received grants to purchase and rehab the greenhouse, several grants to run the CSA, as well as one to write a book on starting an Urban CSA.

We have not had to do very many traditional fundraisers, but when we do, we try to make sure they fit within our values. One fundraiser, to raise funds to buy a rototiller for the CSA, was an evening of music, food, and beer, which the brewing guild in the ecovillage made and donated. Ecovillage residents cooked the food while other residents and friends provided the music. Held in a resident's backyard, the event provided a low cost, wonderful evening of fun and provided the CSA with the funds it needed for the rototiller.

As in most places in our culture, the resources we need are abundant. We strive to take as little as possible and to use these resources in a way that serves the members of the ecovillage, provides meaningful work and involvement, and helps restore this amazing planet. This is what an urban ecovillage offers.

Acquiring Resources: Matt and Elaine Baker Family

Elaine is a vet tech who ran a nonprofit spay and neuter clinic and pet hospice. She worked full time until she and her husband had their first child. They decided they did not want to place their child in daycare, and she wanted to be able to stay home. They started looking at ways to make that happen.

In order to live on one income, they began by simplifying their lives and worked on ways of cutting down expenses. They stopped eating out and now do not do it at all. In the past, with the two of them working full time, it was a regular activity. They sold one of their two cars, and Matt rode his bike 10 miles each way to work at the bike shop. They worked on reducing spending over a three-year time.

Part of reducing spending included moving to the ecovillage because of the following:

- The housing was a lot cheaper.
- They were supported in living frugally.
- They were able to grow a garden and have chickens and goats.
- They concentrated on making things themselves.

• After moving, Matt's bike ride to work was significantly shorter. Instead of a 10-mile ride one way, it was 5 miles.

They moved into the ecovillage in December 2013. By April 2014 Elaine had started an Etsy shop in order to make extra money after quitting her job a year before. She made and sold rings and bracelets. In September, the Etsy business was going so well that Matt was able to scale back at his job. He cut back at work to four days, then just weekends, and eventually quit altogether. Since they simplified, they were able to make enough to live comfortably. Matt says there is only one thing he likes better than running a bike shop, and that is being at home with his kids.

They are continuously looking at ways to simplify their lives. They started homeschooling in 2015 for this reason, but also because they wanted to have the children with them at home.

With a desire to travel, they purchased a used Airstream trailer, and now they can work and homeschool while on the road. They have set up a space to make jewelry in the trailer. All they need is Wi-Fi and a post office, which they can find almost anywhere.

The ecovillage has been a big change for them. Having people around who know each other has been very helpful. Having a community of children has been wonderful, and they love having young people knocking on their door all the time. It makes homeschooling possible because their children have other children to play with in the neighborhood. With like-minded adults around who are Earth-centered and willing to offer a helping hand and/or knowledge has also been a real plus. Also, they are able to travel because they know people who are willing to care for their chickens and goats.

They helped set up the ecovillage's twice-a-week potlucks—just two families at first, and now many people come, and lots of kids play in the yard behind the dining area.

The Baker family's dream for the future of the ecovillage is this:

- Get the urban homesteading store, now in the development stage, up and running
- Have a community meeting place
- Have a place where Matt can work on bikes
- See even more young families move here
- Create more shared projects, such as having a community herd of goats—with a number of people committed to taking care of them
- Work together for more food security through growing more locally with less dependence on food being shipped in from miles away
- See that the ecovillage seeps out into other neighborhoods in Cincinnati and beyond

While the Bakers love it here, there are always ways of improvement, and they are willing to be a part of them.

Elaine and Matt are now carrying out their ultimate dream, forming a rural community. They purchased land with three other couples and have moved there with them.

CHAPTER 8

Food: Producing,
Celebrating & Eating

I grew up on a small 20-acre farm in Southern Indiana. My father sold insurance while my mother and whichever of the 10 children were at home ran the farm. We raised 10,000 chickens per year for market and also had 800 laying hens. The hogs and cattle we raised were primarily for our own consumption of milk and meat, though some of them were also sold.

We had two large gardens. One was a kitchen garden, close to the house, where we grew food we picked often. In the lower garden we grew potatoes, strawberries, corn, and other crops that did not require frequent harvesting.

We ate from the garden during the season and had hundreds of cans of food prepared and stored by the end of the season for the winter months. Before home freezers, we stored our meat in what was called the "locker plant," a location in town that had lockers where townspeople could rent space for storing frozen items. Each week we would take out enough food for that week. Later, a home freezer replaced the lockers. Some items like sugar, salt, and flour we bought at the local IGA grocery store. In all, we raised and stored most of the food that we ate.

From my upbringing, I know that we can grow and preserve the food that we need, but can it be done in an urban area? Throughout our 40 years living on Enright Avenue, I have grown a large garden. However, I did not come close to providing the food that we needed. With Eileen working at various jobs, and me working with Imago, we did not have the time we needed to produce enough food for us to eat year-round. We did can and preserve some of our harvest, which provided a significant amount of our food in the winter. We "put up" bush beans, tomatoes, soups, pear sauce made from our pear tree, and the like.

However, the idea of growing a large amount of food in an urban area was something I felt could be done. A Community Supported Agriculture (CSA) seemed viable in an urban area. After 20 years of considering it and a failed attempt to get one funded through Ben and Jerry's Foundation in 1999, it finally came to fruition. We had a farmer named Charles Griffin living in the ecovillage who had 30 years of CSA growing experience, and a number of residents in the ecovillage were very committed to growing food. Putting these components together, along with my own enthusiasm, the ecovillage CSA was born.

The first year, we used my personal greenhouse attached to my house and five plots totaling a fifth of an acre. With Charles Griffin's skills, we were able to provide enough food for 30 shares. A share provided each person with an equal portion of the food each week for a half year. During our first year we purchased an abandoned greenhouse close to the ecovillage when it became available and had it ready for use by the second year. It had been a commercial florist for over a 100 years. It had closed a few years before.

Since 2009 we have continued the CSA, providing even more shares and using more backyards and lots. During the first five seasons our shareholders would often comment that "We could have used less food." Along the way we received a grant that allowed us to train interns in the urban CSA concept and to develop a book. Two of us worked on the 114-page book titled *Starting Your Urban CSA: A Step-by-Step Guide to Creating a Community-Supported Agriculture Project in Your Urban Neighborhood.*

While there have been many successes, there have also been challenges. A major struggle we have with the CSA is financial. With cheap subsidized food in our supermarkets, it is hard to compete without subsidies. Even though people appreciated the amount and the quality of the CSA shares, it is also very difficult to get people to pay what the food is really worth. In our society we are so used to paying a very small percentage of our income on the factory-farmed food we can so easily purchase. Consequently, we find it really hard to spend more, even for quality food. The CSA has been subsidized with some grants, donations, and through ecovillage funds, and this will probably be a continued need. But the food has been excellent, and we have provided farmers with work doing what they love to do. Regardless, we have established a CSA community that is exciting and viable. About a third of the CSA members come from the ecovillage, the rest from surrounding neighborhoods.

Because we use many backyards and lots, one of our challenges is the quality of the soil. The soil in each garden is different, thus requiring the farmers to be very conscious of the soil types to determine what will grow best. There is a constant effort to make compost, which requires gathering material from various places as well as collecting kitchen scraps from members, restaurants, coffee shops, and grocery stores. We are able to compost near each of the backyard lots, but there are some restrictions around large-scale composting in the city. We occasionally receive compost from groups that are willing to share. Some of us are interested in doing research around different types of compost and what works best in our urban gardens.

We are thankful that the CSA is so successful; interestingly, each year it runs a few shares short of its projected goal. Improving our marketing strategy should solve this problem.

Food Production in the Ecovillage

Eileen and I have given our garden space to the CSA, so we have a very small garden area where we still grow some of our food. Others have their own gardens in their backyards as well. These provide great food, but also an opportunity for people to touch the soil and connect with the non-human world in a wonderful dance of caring and consumption.

While these gardens are a major source of food for some in the ecovillage, there are many other diverse ways of food production. Several families raise other things, such as goats, chickens, ducks, and bees. So far, these are for personal consumption and do not provide for the larger community. The CSA built a chicken coop at its greenhouse that provided eggs for shareholders until a weasel broke through and killed the flock. Another enterprising person even tried to start spores for growing mushrooms at the greenhouse. Some people are growing hops for the brew guild. Four families participate in a chicken co-op, sharing the cleaning, feeding, and gathering of eggs. There are a variety of creative ideas for producing as much food in the ecovillage as possible.

Two families joined together to grow a large amount of food in their backyards so that they could sell food at a local farmers market. The food is grown in large backyards with the growing space wrapping around into their front yards. They also have animals that provide manure for fertilizing their gardens. While they did well selling at the farmers market, they have recently decided they can use most of the food they grow themselves and for the CSA. The CSA, this family, and most of the gardens in the ecovillage grow their food using organic methods.

Preserving food is something many families do. While canning is a popular method, some people dry their food, others freeze it, and still others use fermentation. All practices are done on an individual basis. We have not developed a community effort in this regard as of yet.

A few years ago, a number of residents joined together to create a Forest Garden at the Imago Earth Center, others in their backyards. They planted fruit and nut trees, berries, and perennials that one finds in and around some woods. In our area, persimmons, elderberry, pecans, walnuts, pawpaws, raspberries, blackberries and the like can make up the Forest Garden. This will be both a productive garden and provide food for the CSA as well as a demonstration project.

There is no significant foraging in the ecovillage, though there has been a great deal of discussion about it. One family harvested black walnuts from the surrounding woods, hulled them and sold them—but decided not to repeat this effort because it is so time consuming. They now do it just for themselves. The Imago Earth Center has hosted a Mulberry Festival in June, when a large number of Mulberry trees in the ecovillage are ripe. Individuals made Mulberry cheesecake, muffins, salads, jams, ice cream, beer, etc. Samples were offered too, and the food was judged by those who came. I won one year with my mulberry ice cream.

Fruit trees have been planted for the CSA around its garden areas: peaches, plums, apples, elderberry, pawpaw. We have also planted fruit trees in honor of people who have died. This is a wonderful way of celebrating a life, one that will literally bear fruit for years.

Other Ways of Accessing Food

Deborah Jordan, an active member of the ecovillage, started a food guide for this region called the Central Ohio River Valley Guide (CORV) that is a wonderful resource for the broader community. Imago served as the fiscal agent for the guide for a number of years, and the ecovillage CSA has been highlighted in the guide.

To complement produce from the CSA, we also started a food-buying club in the ecovillage. Every four weeks we order food from a natural and organic wholesaler and distribute it to co-op members. We do still purchase food at grocery stores oriented to healthy food, as well as using the supermarket that is just up the street.

I've mentioned this in earlier chapters, so it should be no surprise that we embrace food-sharing via potlucks. They are integral to our ecovillage experience because they are an easy way for us to connect to one another. In the beginning, the Reidels made their backyards and homes available for potlucks two evenings per week. There is also a yearly chili and dessert cook-off, and many other excuses to get together to share meals. The potluck has been moved to Common Roots Pub, which has become something of a center for the ecovillage. Some of us dream of a common house—in addition to Common Roots and Imago Earth Center where we will gather more frequently.

We have varied food preferences in the ecovillage. There are carnivores, vegetarians, and vegans. At our bi-weekly potlucks there is an array of soups, salads, stews, and vegetables. There are also main dishes, some of them with meat mostly grown in the ecovillage or by local farmers. Gluten-free choices are also available. The meals are so varied that almost anyone's diet can be accommodated.

I developed my own preference after being a vegetarian for five years. I became a vegetarian because of the way animals are treated in our culture. After a number of years, it dawned on me that not only are animals treated poorly, but the way vegetables are grown is also unacceptable. I have long believed that not only animals are sentient, but plants are as well. Therefore, it is more important to me to consider how our food is grown, harvested, prepared, and eaten rather than the types of food we eat. All our food needs to be produced and eaten with deep respect for the life that is being offered, whether plant or animal. Eileen's and my diet have evolved to being almost completely organic. While a food may be declared organic, it does not guarantee that it was grown in a respectful way, though there is a better possibility that it was. We do not eat a great deal of meat, but it is in our diet.

I look forward to the time when the forest gardens will produce in abundance for both human animals and other animals in the eco-village. I would also like to see us share even more meals together. I dream of a time when most of the food we eat is raised in the ecovillage.

Food: Suellyn Shupe

Food came first. Suellyn cooked meals for a family of five for thirty years. While being somewhat aware of proper nutrition through her nursing education, she used mostly commercial foods. She also grew some things, flowers, and tomatoes mostly. In 1997 she became involved with Grailville, a community of women living sustainably in Loveland, Ohio, where, when she divorced, she became part of an organic garden internship for four months. She lived there and worked on their CSA. She became a member of the Ohio Ecological Food and Farm Association (OEFFA).

After a friend attended a permaculture session at the annual OEFFA conference in 2004, the two of them decided to take a permaculture design course in Stelle, Illinois. Here she learned a set of design principles centered on sustainable and self-sufficient systems thinking which utilizes the patterns observed in natural eco-systems. She also attended a teacher training course with Peter Bane in 2008 at Grailville. After that, along with two other teachers, she began teaching courses on permaculture.

She had heard about the ecovillage. Trina Paulus, a Grail member, called her one day in 2008 and said she was going to look at some houses in the ecovillage, and asked if Suellyn wanted to go along. She had been thinking of looking for a house but had not begun doing so. On this visit they viewed the house Suellyn eventually bought in April 2008 and where she now lives. She remembers the date because shortly after she bought it the Cincinnati Permaculture Institute held their first permaculture design course at her new 100-year-old house.

Suellyn chose to live in the ecovillage not only because of the house itself, but also because of its location. She wanted a place where she could live permanently and safely as an older single woman. Mostly she wanted to be with like-minded people who participate in sustainable living practices. She already knew people in the ecovillage who lived sustainably, so it was an easy choice. She quickly got to know a large number of the people in the community.

It was a good move for her. She finds it very entertaining because there is always something to do. If you stay home people will either seek you out or leave you alone whatever you want. More young people have moved here, which is a good and fun thing. She feels the ecovillage has changed goals and activities, such as moving away from rehabbing houses and toward developing a CSA but without changing its general mission.

The CSA Project was one long-range goal to which Suellyn became committed. In the fall of 2008 when a group of people with a deep interest in food came together to discuss starting a CSA in the ecovillage, Suellyn threw herself into the idea. With real enthusiasm, she became the coordinator of the CSA for the next three years. Following that, she became the chair of the CSA. She has now stepped down from that position but remains an active participant and shareholder.

Her suggestion to people interested in becoming involved in food issues is to grow something to eat. One can get caught up in reading best gardening practices or politics surrounding food, but if a person grows something, he or she will be hooked. It is encouraging to see who else is growing and how it affects the total food economy, and it also demonstrates that there is a great deal of work to do. The best place to start is to grow, prepare, and eat food.

CHAPTER 9

Housing

A Short History

We began Imago in 1978 as a nonprofit ecological education organization doing programs in the community because of growing environmental concerns. Initially we focused on encouraging people to transform their neighborhoods to become greener. We intuitively knew what science is now proving: that connecting with nature makes people happier. We were also aware that we needed to live more sustainably as a way to preserve the planet we are totally dependent on. We tried many different paths: programs around simple living, energy conservation, and studying spiritual leaders such as Thomas Berry. Early on we attracted many local as well as national speakers to Imago.

While we were offering workshops, we decided that we needed to "walk our talk." A small group of Imago members began planning what this might look like. We decided to focus on Price Hill, the Cincinnati neighborhood where we all lived.

In the mid 1990's we began with a neighborhood housing survey. We wanted to ascertain the home ownership rate and the condition of the housing stock. Our research showed that Price Hill, one of Cincinnati's largest neighborhoods, had a high ownership rate and the structures were in generally good shape. To support our efforts to enhance the green nature of the neighborhood, we held annual garden festivals promoting the planting of street trees, home vegetable gardens, and tours of the best green efforts in the neighborhood. We also brought to these celebrations well-known experts who held workshops teaching others best practices.

However, our efforts were not enough to buck the national housing trend. There was a noticeable decline in the condition of the housing stock and an increase in the number of foreclosures in Price Hill.

In late 1997 a coalition of charitable foundations led by the Greater Cincinnati Foundation, offered a half-million dollar grant over five years to two city neighborhoods. Their goal was to see neighborhood revitalization efforts using Comprehensive Community development techniques.

I wrote a proposal for this grant through Imago that offered a plan to develop an ecovillage in East Price Hill, and Imago was awarded the grant. However, our initial effort to form an ecovillage was not successful. The neighborhood we chose to work in was too large, it was the most depressed area in Price Hill, and we did not have a support system there to help us develop it. We did create a comprehensive community development organization called Price Hill Will. The western part of the city did not have a community development organization at the time. With the housing crisis in full swing, Price Hill needed such an organization

In Price Hill, as in many neighborhoods across the country, there were numerous foreclosures and absentee landlords. One of the most horrendous tactics was the lease-option-to-buy scams. Houses that needed crucial repairs were sold to people who could not get a conventional loan to buy a house. The scam consisted of taking a large down payment, and then charging large monthly payments with a percentage going toward the purchase. Frequently people had to make repairs, such as replacing a furnace, and when they did, they could not afford to make the house payments. The scam worked to evict people when they were in arrears of their monthly payments. Sometimes houses were leased two or more times to different families in one year in order to capture the down payment. Many low-income families were hurt by this.

Housing in the Ecovillage:

In 2004, Price Hill Will separated from Imago and became an independent organization that continues to do good work for the larger neighborhood. This same year Imago focused on forming an ecovillage on Enright Avenue. There were already many people who had moved to Enright Avenue because of Imago. As mentioned in earlier chapters, it seemed an easy transition to start a smaller, more intimate ecovillage where like-minded people were already gathering.

Housing was one of the main issues that the ecovillage members began to address. Rehabbing houses took on a priority as fore-closures began to hit Enright Avenue. The ecovillage had a policy of only buying houses susceptible to speculators who wanted only to make money on the houses without concern for their condition. This means we never bought houses selling at market rate because we felt assured that buyers of these homes would live in them and take care of them. When a house became available that the ecovillage wanted to see saved, we first tried to find someone interested in living in the ecovillage to buy and rehab it. If this did not happen, in collaboration with Imago, we would buy the house and renovate it to be a more ecologically responsible home. Imago used sustainable methods in rehabbing, including extensive insulation, energy-efficient heating and cooling, water conservation, and efficient lighting. Subsequently, most of these houses were sold to people interested in being part of the ecovillage. We retained a few to provide rental apartments for people who wanted to move to the ecovillage but who could not afford to purchase.

The ecovillage's efforts to rehab houses and sell them eventually expanded to twenty-five houses. Some of them were on streets just east of Enright Avenue. The ecovillage expanded its boundaries and housing rehab to include McPherson Avenue, Terry Street, and Wells Street, using the same plan and resources. Our rehab policy was to sell the homes at approximately the same price as was invested in them; our profit margin was very slim, but gaining a profit was not our goal.

Financing Housing Purchases

When I worked as a coordinator with Price Hill Will, I had set up a relationship with the Hubert Foundation. Through this foundation we had the funds we needed to purchase and rehab houses. When Imago wanted to buy a house, the Hubert Foundation would lend us the money. Imago repaid the foundation the principal owed, plus zero to three percent interest when it sold the house. Imago also employed contractors who were willing to work on its houses at a reduced rate. Volunteers were also an important part of renovation efforts. With this, Imago was able to sell the homes and break even. When the ecovillage acquired its tax-exempt status, it took over the purchase and rehab of houses in the ecovillage from Imago with the financial help from the Hubert Foundation transferring to the ecovillage.

We vastly improved the housing stock and attracted home-owners committed to sustainable green living. Our strategy for selling houses involved showcasing the eco-neighborhood. We did this through monthly tours, social media, and email lists from both Imago and the ecovillage.

In all, Imago and the ecovillage have been able to sell all the houses they purchased except for two properties retained for rentals. The rent from these provides the ecovillage with some of the small amount of finances needed to operate.

More than Housing

In 2009 the ecovillage purchased a former florist shop that included a retail space. It came with two greenhouses and a vacant lot for the CSA program. In June of 2015 we purchased a bar that had been having a negative effect on the neighborhood. The property came with an indoor bar and retail space, a large outdoor beer garden, and a second-floor apartment. We use the pub as a gathering place for the ecovillage and the broader community, a place to share information about green living and as a location for entertainment.

The ecovillage also owns and manages the Burr Oak Building, an apartment with five units and a commercial space. This building is fully rented with the retail space occupied by the Cincinnati Zen Center.

In 2010 the ecovillage board decided to focus their time and energy on the CSA and the buildings they presently owned and managed and decided not to continue rehabbing and selling houses. Consequently, another nonprofit organization, Community Earth Alliance, accepted this responsibility and has rehabbed 10 additional houses with the aid of the Hubert Foundation.

Housing has been an exciting and successful program in the ecovillage. It has removed significant blight and attracted new residents interested in being part of the ecovillage. These new residents are participating in the leadership of the community and providing strategic planning. In addition, they have brought delightful benefits to the ecovillage, including children, chicken, goats, and a love for Earth.

Housing: Megan and Dan Divelbiss

Megan and Dan are not Cincinnati natives. They moved separately to the city to attend college. Megan studied at the art academy, then became an AmeriCorps volunteer for Imago. Through this she became interested in nature mentoring and became a certified Waldorf teacher. Dan went to the University of Cincinnati and received a master's degree in environmental engineering. He was interested in water issues and worked with Engineers Without Borders in Guatemala for three years. After Dan returned from Guatemala, he and Megan met at the Rohs Street Cafe near U.C. and began dating.

Both grew up in the country but enjoyed living in cities. They had a desire for some of the attributes of country living (a little land, space where they could have animals, along with neighbors "hip" to these ideas). Megan worked in the ecovillage while at Imago and became excited to see folks in different stages of life who were in a similar arc as she was. The ecovillage offered a mix of young families, people in mid-career, people approaching retirement, and those already retired who had an ecological awareness and wanted to reflect it in their lifestyle. It felt like a healthy and encouraging place to put down roots.

Shortly after they were engaged, Megan heard about a house for sale in the ecovillage. It turned out to be a well-preserved and perfect house for them. They became only the third owners of this century-old house, which was built right before World War I. They did not know the first owner, but assume it was a German family since there are planks in the house with German writing. It has an acre and a half of land, some woods, and a good-sized yard with enough room to have animals. They could even have a few alpacas if they wanted.

They love the geography of the street and the land. When they look out the back door of their home, they do not see any houses, they see just beautiful backyards and woods. With the way things were laid out, they knew there would never be any large developments near them. Plus, it is in the city, just minutes from downtown, and close to many services.

When Megan saw the house, she said out loud that it would be a perfect place for a school with the layout of the house and the land. This continued to be on her mind as she completed her Waldorf education and then taught at a Waldorf School. She stopped teaching at the school when their daughter was born. Megan stayed home with their daughter and prepared to start a preschool Waldorf program, which she did when her daughter reached two years old. Her preschool serves ages two to six, with a possibility of kindergarten in the future.

They have completed a great deal of work on the house. They have insulated the whole structure, made parts of the house more functional for them, such as expanding the kitchen since they love to cook, and building a deck for children to play. There are still many energy-efficient projects they envision for the space. They are anxious to have a solar water heater and photovoltaics.

The ecovillage has served them well. When they first moved here, they jumped into a number of activities. However, with a new home, new jobs, and the arrival of their daughter, they realized they were too actively involved and had to withdraw. Once things settle down, they want to re-engage, volunteering on a smaller scale to begin with. They continue to enjoy the healthy interaction with people in the neighborhood and know that wonderful things are happening.

They are excited to see more families move into the ecovillage. They want to be more involved in the CSA, potlucks, Imago, and participating in Earth rituals. They also want to tap into the food-buying co-op and the Common Roots homesteading store as a way to collectively source more of their food and other items to receive bulk pricing at affordable rates.

They envision more skill-sharing among members in the community such as yoga, massage, sewing, raising small livestock, water sanitation, and construction. Many of their dreams have come true. Megan started a Waldorf preschool which she runs from her home. Dan began a hydroponics vegetable growing business that has proved to be very successful.

While much of this is part of a dream, they feel it is all a real possibility. They plan to be in their home for years and want to make their dreams come true through the ecovillage.

CHAPTER 10

Children in the Ecovillage

A Short History of Children Living on Enright Avenue

Our own children, Devin and Megan, grew up before the ecovillage was established, though we had begun to form a community in the neighborhood. Throughout the late 1970s and through the 1980s we had other adults living in our home with us. We also had a group of people who ate together every evening except Sundays. Although Devin and Megan were the only children in the group, the adults at these dinners provided them with a great deal of love and information that has followed them through life. Among these life lessons was a deep sense of commitment and love for Earth. While our children spent a great deal of time playing with other youngsters on the street, none of the other families with children participated in these community dinners or had an ecological commitment.

In past years there would be phases of either a majority of girls in the neighborhood or a majority of boys. When my children were young, we went through a "boy" phase, so Devin spent hours and hours with other boys playing in the woods surrounding the ecovillage. Megan had only a few friends on the street, none of whom were her age.

There were some typical events with children in the ecovillage. One was an annual "TP"ing of the trees that ran along Enright Avenue on "damage night," the night before Halloween Eve. Some people were bothered by this, but most enjoyed it. The streamers in the morning, especially on foggy days, were wonderful. The toilet paper was biodegradable, and this act was quite harmless to individuals and property. This had started many years before we moved to the street and continued for many years.

Because Enright Avenue is on a dead end with little traffic, playing basketball on the street also began years ago. The children used a basketball hoop extending from the front yard of a home to practice or to have games. When a car came, they respectfully moved aside to let it through, never giving drivers a hard time. Although some people objected to this, I did not see any problem with it; they are on the street where they can be seen, which means they are not doing any damage anywhere else. What can be wrong with that?

We also spent time involving many of the children on Enright Avenue in ecologically oriented events. They helped us plant street trees not only on Enright, but throughout Price Hill as part of a Cincinnati Urban Forestry effort to reforest Cincinnati. We planted fifty trees per year over a five-year period and could not have done this without the children's help. Our 250 trees were among the 4000 planted in Price Hill by Urban Forestry.

In 1993 Imago bought an eight-acre parcel of land along Enright Avenue where we began offering programs for school children and Scouts, as well as summer programs for children. Each year thousands of children came from throughout the city to experience nature in the city with programs on topics like insects, seed dispersal, and gardening. Imago also became a place where children on Enright became involved, especially during the summer camps, first as participants and later as counselors.

Two women who had been Girl Scouts started a Girl Scout-type program. They called it the "Girl's Club." They met with the girls on a regular basis, involving them in a variety of indoor and outdoor activities, such as games, trekking in the woods, and campfire cooking.

The natural world became familiar to the children in the ecovillage, and Imago became part of their backyard. The neighborhood became a friendly place to be. When the ecovillage began, it was not a big surprise that the children already had some sense of what it meant to live in community and to care about the Earth.

Ecovillage Draws Young Families

Once the ecovillage officially became an entity, young families began migrating to it. It was a place they saw where they could live with others who cared about the Earth, and also where they could raise their children with like-minded families. Now there are over two dozen children from 6 months to 16 years old. We have had home births in the ecovillage, but more often families go to hospitals for childbirth. Families feel supported with whatever choice they make. There is a wonderful tolerance for people's child-rearing choices here in the ecovillage.

Today, children are involved in many events with the ecovillage. Families come together to sled on snowy days, to ride bikes, to go into the woods, and to gather for potlucks, and we always welcome the children. They find these gatherings normal. All children, regardless of whether or not their parents are invested in the ecovillage, are encouraged to participate.

One of the most advantageous aspects of living here has been the availability of childcare. Children are invited to spend the day or night with a family, which frees up parents for activities they have a hard time accomplishing with children underfoot. There are a number of families who willingly watch children. They frequently gain as well, with their own children occupied and engaged with visiting children. It is often a win-win situation.

However, there are differences in parenting styles. While most parents welcome other adults correcting their children, there are varying degrees in strictness, in ways of communicating to children, in how late they can be out, and the like. While this sometimes affects the parents' decisions about who watches their children, there have been few disagreements thus far. Instead, there seems to be a trust and sense of tolerance among parents.

During the twice-weekly potlucks and all-member meetings, parents have a real opportunity to participate in conversations with other adults as their children are off playing together in an area where they can be observed. These also give childless adults a chance to observe and interact with the children. While this may fulfill their maternal/paternal instincts, it also meets a need in the children to be cared for. They realize there are other adults in the neighborhood who care about them, who care about what they think, and are available if they ever need guidance or assistance.

Education in the Ecovillage

The schooling experience also varies widely. Some people home-school, a good number go to private schools like the Waldorf school, others attend magnet schools within the Cincinnati public school system, and some go to regular public or parochial schools. Since there is strong support for learning, children are usually successful wherever they spend their school years.

We have four parents from different families trained as Waldorf teachers, with two of them currently teaching at the local Waldorf school. Megan Divelbiss opened her Waldorf preschool in the fall of 2017 on Enright Avenue. Since the Waldorf philosophy emphasizes the role of imagination in learning, striving to holistically integrate the intellectual, practical, and artistic development of pupils, it does seem compatible with the ecovillage philosophy. The woods surrounding us provide an ideal place for children to wander and experience nature. In the larger culture, this may be discouraged among many parents fearful of the "wild," though it is encouraged among most parents committed to the ecovillage and to those who send their children to Waldorf Schools.

A big part of Megan Divelbiss's Waldorf preschool program is giving children an opportunity to experience the natural world while spending a part of every day outside. Some of the other Waldorf educators have talked of starting a regular Waldorf school within the ecovillage boundaries, but this may be some years in the future.

Being Part of the Ecovillage

Even though our own children did not grow up in the organized ecovillage, they continue living with a sense of awe with the Earth and work to share this with their children. As adults, they do not live in the ecovillage, though they have remained close to us, remaining in Cincinnati. Our daughter is a librarian, and our son works in wetland restoration. Their children love the outdoors, and the older ones are deeply concerned about what is happening to the planet.

Children (and grandchildren) are also encouraged to be involved in ecovillage projects. Sometimes they help by cutting grass or by working in the CSA greenhouse. The older kids help with childcare during ecovillage events. Almost all of them enjoy caring for animals and participating in Imago's programs. It is wonderful to see children exhibiting a sense of responsibility and purpose in these activities.

One of the things that makes me appreciate the children even more is when I hear them responding to environmental degradation in ways that communicate their displeasure. They can be vocal during movie nights when the problems with plastic bags or water issues are presented. A five-year-old recently said to the group attending the film that he thinks all cars with smoke pouring out of their tailpipes should be crushed "because that's not good for the Earth." Children also react to trash thrown into the street. There is not a lot in the ecovillage, but when there is, I have heard a sigh of disgust from a child who then proceeded to pick it up to discard it in an appropriate container. To treat the Earth with respect is becoming part of these children's culture.

Many families emphasize non-mainstream ways of living. Some join together in making presents for birthdays and other gift-giving holidays rather than purchasing them. This appeals especially to pre-teens. There are stresses in families, especially during the teenage years, as children feel a real need to "fit in." And living alternatively can be a challenge for ecovillage children, which can make it challenging for families with teenage children. For example, parents may not allow their children to have access to television, smartphones, or the like, or when they do, it is on a very limited basis. The children may wear used rather than new clothes, which can be in stark contrast to their teenage friends. Such stress is something that each family needs to work out on their own since there is no simple solution. On the other hand, teens enjoy the opportunity to babysit and do other tasks for people in the ecovillage to earn some spending money. This is a real perk to living in the ecovillage.

Due to strong values connected with communication styles, cooperative living, and respect for the Earth, we anticipate that children who grow up in the ecovillage will be well-adjusted and capable of interacting successfully in whatever situation they encounter. We believe that having experienced a deep connection to Earth, living in community and living more self-sufficiently will also prepare them for an uncertain future.

Children: Elizabeth Doshi

Elizabeth worked with children for most of her life. When she was 10 and living in Norwell, Massachusetts, she started babysitting for the family next door. It was the 1970s and her neighborhood was filled with children. Her family alone had seven kids, and because four of her siblings were younger than she, her neighbors were confident in Elizabeth's care for their two boys. At night she told them stories about dragons or wizards or something fantastic. She became close to this family, and when it was time for her to go to college, they helped pay for her first two years at a very prestigious university in New York.

Her childhood was ideal. She ran in the woods behind her house with siblings and friends. They walked to the candy store, an hour away. They rode bikes and horses down a dirt road to the local recreation building that was used for clambakes in the summer. They built forts and turned over logs to find salamanders.

All of this led to her interest in teaching and becoming certified as a Waldorf teacher. A teaching position at the Cincinnati Waldorf School led her to move to Cincinnati. She purposely moved to the ecovillage in the summer of 2012 with her daughter, an only child. It was her hope, which came to fruition, that she would be able to raise chickens, plant a garden, and have a house they could afford without having to sacrifice time spent with family and community.

She felt comfortable letting her seven-year-old daughter leave the house to play with friends down the street because of the community of people in the ecovillage. Having come from a rural area, she did not expect this in an urban setting. When they went outside their house, it was the norm to see people they knew. Or if they went for a walk, they would often stop and chat with friends or pet a familiar dog. In fact, it was hard for them to go anywhere in the ecovillage and not see a friend. Conversations were always waiting to begin.

One aspect of her childhood is very different from her daughter's childhood. When Elizabeth was growing up, she knew children, but not adults, and almost everyone on her street was wealthy, Christian, and Caucasian. Because of the diversity of the ecovillage neighborhood, her daughter knows families with different economic, cultural, ethnic, and religious backgrounds. Elizabeth and her daughter like to socialize with ecovillage members, both adults, and children. Having so many adults on the street for guidance and inspiration allows her daughter the opportunity to grow with a diverse array of influences. It seems to balance her and make her feel like she belongs. They eat dinner with other families each week and share in taking care of each other's children.

Similar to her own childhood, Elizabeth's daughter has a connection with the natural world. Their home is near the Imago Earth Center. They participate with Imago in the care of the forest that surrounds the neighborhood. Elizabeth's daughter participates in Imago camps and plays in its woods. She enjoys tenting with her friends in their backyard near the forest. Because the Earth is valued, she and her friends take its needs and preferences quite seriously. Being in the woods, caring for plants and animals, feeding the birds in the winter are examples of their deep care and love for the Earth.

It helps Elizabeth that most of the parents who participate in helping the ecovillage have a similar parenting approach. Screen-time is limited and being on the outside of the screen door is encouraged. Spending time together with other parents, sharing projects, discussing childcare and books they've read—these are things that Elizabeth values a great deal. With the huge backyards, the children can play while she spends time with the other parents.

Her daughter is not secluded from the broader urban community. She attends the Waldorf school and interacts with other children at the local library and pool. Because of this, she is learning that the world is beautifully full of all kinds of people and that the measure of a person has very little to do with what can be seen on the surface but what intentions they carry.

CHAPTER 11

Play

At Enright Ridge Urban Ecovillage, we believe in play. The Oxford Dictionary defines play as "Engag[ing] in activity for enjoyment and recreation rather than a serious or practical purpose." While I agree with the first part, I have trouble with the second half of the definition because I believe our culture needs to see play as integral to our lifestyles, and that means taking it seriously and doing it practically for the betterment of our health and happiness. Helen and Scott Nearing discuss this in their book *Living the Good Life*. They explain that in some indigenous cultures, people spend half their time working and the rest of their time in leisure, in what might be called play. They themselves followed this idea in their own lives by working part of the day in survival tasks such as growing food, managing the land, and shelter upkeep; the other part of their days they spent in their version of leisure by writing, spending time teaching at their homestead, and playing music. Play and work are not opposites; play can actually be part of our work life and our work lives can be part of play. We have the potential to enjoy the work we do and do it as a form of play. It keeps us sane and can make the tasks we undertake not just bearable but enjoyable.

I still struggle in my own life with the notion of play as being legitimate. I grew up in a family where my mother woke at 6 a.m. and worked till she went to bed at 10 p.m. Since there were six children at home, she prepared three large meals a day and made most of our clothing. We also grew most of our own food. There was little time for her even to read. We had most of Sunday off, except for the necessary work of feeding animals and milking the cow. We played a lot as young children, but as we grew older, we started to work more on the farm by helping to grow, harvest, and cook the food we ate. We went to school and did homework in the evening. We worked hard and we never questioned it. It was the way we lived.

My days now look entirely different from my life on the farm. Since I left my job as a social worker in the late 1970s and helped start Imago, my work has equaled play. I still work as hard as I did on the farm, though I love what I do. While I may easily put in more than 40 hours per week, I tend to view it through a lens of play because I love talking to people, giving presentations, programming Earth-centered events, and helping rehab houses to make them more energy-efficient. Although stressful and challenging things have happened, and sometimes I really did not like what I had to do, most of the time my work life has been play. It has been enjoyable and a constant sense of recreation. Joe Dominguez, in his book *Your Money or Your Life*, says that most people do not work for a living but work for a dying. If people work for a living, they should come home in the evening charged up and alive. However, most people do not like the job they have and come home burned out—in other words, they've been "working for a dying." I have been honored to be able to work for a living, having fun each day doing what I love.

Admittedly, having very little interest in money has helped me do what I love. For most of my career, the larger culture has not supported the kind of work I do, but as more people are becoming ecologically minded, I am able to see the fruits of my labor. And it is good to see a greater sense of awareness not only for the Earth, but also for the concept of play or the work/play connection. I have come around to see that in this connection we can truly enjoy what we do and have fun doing it.

In the ecovillage, we often try to combine work and play and have the same type of joy and excitement. For example, when we started the ecovillage a group of us built a trail in the woods around it. It was hard work, but it was also playful. We had to bushwhack our way through the underbrush to figure out the direction the trail was going to take, figure out what plants and logs needed to be removed, and remove or prune the obstacles with clippers and saws. It was an activity I loved. It is the sharing of this type of experience that is play for me. I can do things alone like garden, for example, and experience the playfulness of it. However, working in a group can be especially playful for me.

Another way the ecovillage combined work and play was in a campaign not to use plastic bags for a month. In 2016 some 20 households pledged to avoid them. It was fun talking to people about how they did it, including some of the difficulties and the exhilaration in not using plastic. There was a great deal of laughter about the struggles people had getting cashiers not to use plastic bags, but we also shared great ideas for explaining to them why we brought our own bags. My family has continued this practice as have most people who took the month-long pledge. It was playful, while being a serious commitment.

Of course, we also play without work involved, and one of the most frequent ways we do this in the ecovillage is the potluck dinners. Both adults and children find opportunities to relax and have a good time; the children wander off by themselves to play, which gives the adults time to share recipes or a bottle of wine, to playfully tease, to share friendly and meaningful discussions and learning. Sometimes we have special potlucks, such as a cheese, chocolate, and wine potluck. I do not find our potlucks much different in many ways from potlucks I experienced growing up, though the difference is in the frequency, the organic and locally grown food, and in the conversations that support me in my attempts to live a more sustainable life. The laidback nature, the bantering, and people's stories about their everyday life experiences make these potlucks truly fun events.

Maybe one of the easiest ways to play is through shared stories; I believe we as a people love stories. It is a way we learn, but also a way we find joy in the activities around us. For example, it is both interesting and enjoyable to listen and talk with people about their installation of solar panels, their challenges and successes as gardeners, their experiences bicycling on city streets, their planting of milkweed for Monarch butterflies or of putting in a forest garden. Stories are in many cases much fun and a joy to listen to, while also offering a challenge to try a particular experience oneself.

Then there is the traditional meaning of play. I love watching young ones—humans, dogs, cats, etc. —playing. They become totally engrossed in an undertaking that also teaches them life skills. They develop not only motor skills, but also communicating and relating skills. This type of play is a very human thing to do, and it needs no excuse, though we do need to allow for more playtime for adults as well. While our larger culture can sometimes make adults feel silly or guilty for play, we in the ecovillage make a conscious effort to support our members and our neighbors in activities that give them joy. In an article in *Psychology Today* (May 2014), Rob Parr says that "Recreational deprivation has been linked to criminality, obesity, and declining creativity." He asks why having fun is not taken more seriously. "Play is a banquet for the brain, a smorgasbord for the senses, providing nourishment for body and spirit: sad then that as a society we seem to be starving ourselves of it."

We are not starving in the ecovillage. Our members do many of the same recreational things as many people. We have a basketball hoop on the street. It is not unusual for an impromptu game of football or baseball to spring up on the street. It is fun to be a part of it and fun to watch. Some people are into disc golf. We also bowl, garden, read and share books, and have lively book discussions, among many other things.

Perhaps the activity that is most prevalent in the ecovillage is hiking in the woods, in groups or individually. Sometimes I struggle with allowing myself to walk in the woods on a regular basis, thanks to my upbringing. I have worked with others preparing the paths around the ecovillage, making it possible to enter the world of other species. I try to spend time each day in the woods, listening to the other species that make up our community. When I allow myself to do so, it is truly a sense of play, of wonder, of connecting with what is important in life, communing with other members of the community. The animals and plants are there ready to play. I just have to allow myself the opportunity.

Another unique aspect of our ecovillage is that we have our own pub. Going to or being part of open mic night is a hoot. The music can be amazing. Poetry and standup add to the entertainment on mic night. On other nights I've enjoyed drumming events, sing-alongs, contra-dancing and concerts. The tables end up in many different configurations depending on the event. This is local enter-tainment at its best. We also have drinks that are environmentally sensitive. In purchasing liquor for the bar, our priorities are 1) local/organic, 2) local, 3) organic, then 4) conventional. With this lineup of drinks, we have the greenest bar in Cincinnati!

Taking time out to play and to have fun is incredibly important. Even when our culture does not see it as important, recreation really is a re-creation, and we need to put play and fun into our every-day lives to re-create ourselves. While I love to travel, enjoy playing sports, and appreciate going to plays and music events, they are not necessary. I can go for months without such encounters and still have a great deal of joy in my life because play and fun are part it. I find this frame of mind among many residents of the ecovillage.

So, let's play. It is a great mantra for our times. It is a way that the ecovillage takes on the serious business of creating an urban setting that can serve our cities and have fun doing it.

Play: Michael Frazier and Kim Brown

Michael was born and grew up in Cincinnati. After high school he went to Anderson University in Indiana. Kim was born and raised in Fox River Grove, Illinois, a small rural town. She grew up near a nature preserve and river and enjoyed being outside as a child. She also went to Anderson University after high school, where she met Michael in her freshman year. After college they moved to Cincinnati. Michael works at Northern Kentucky University as a graphic designer. After attending graduate school in Social Work, Kim worked at Focus on Youth as a play therapist.

It is no accident that she became a registered Play Therapist and that play became a part of her social work position. Kim believes play is a universal language in which anyone of any age can participate. She knows play has many benefits: relieving stress, increasing creativity and problem solving, boosting one's mood, providing opportunities to socialize and connect with others, and keeping people feeling young and energetic. Kim remained at Focus on Youth until she left her job in 2015 to be home with Henna, their daughter. This also allows her to do work she chooses with a lot less stress and a lot more joy.

In 2004 Kim and Michael began looking for an older house. Price Hill was one of the few neighborhoods where they could afford buying the type of home they desired. While they did not know much about the neighborhood, they realized Imago's Earth Center was close by. This was a major incentive in buying their home. They

found it online and bought it from Imago. Then they began learning about the neighborhood and were part of the 2004 meeting that
started the ecovillage, where they were excited to meet people with
shared interests.

They came to the neighborhood with an interest in ecology,
energy-saving, farming, food, and architecture, but they did not have
much experience. With their interest in architecture, they helped
build a small straw-bale building in the ecovillage for a resident
needing extra space.

Along with these interests they have a desire for a strong sense
of community. Although Kim grew up in a small town and under-
stands the value of close relationships, Michael did not realize he
would enjoy a close-knit community because he grew up in a neighborhood where he did not know many people. He quickly came to
realize how wonderful it is to relate to the people in the ecovillage.
When he goes to the grocery store, he always knows someone there.
He and Kim enjoy going to the corner bar for a drink among friends.

As part of the planning to start the ecovillage, they offered to host
a weekly game night. We have gathered at their house in different
seasons for games of frisbee or croquet in their backyard, for board
games in the depth of winter, and for riotous games of Charades or
Pictionary during any season. This tradition has carried on since the
beginning of the ecovillage, and it now includes their young daughter Henna, who also enjoys the gatherings for fun and games.

Michael and Kim cherish the playful time they spend with family
and friends and especially enjoy being outside, hiking in the woods.
Even urban hiking has become an important part of their lives. They
load Henna into her stroller and wandering off to the nearby coffee
shop, playgrounds or library are great times. They also enjoy sports:
disc golf, swimming at the nearby parks, and bowling.

At the top of their "playlist" is music. They love live music, and
it is one of the common denominators that brought them together.

Living in Cincinnati provides them with a great venue for it. They truly love Imago's Music in the Woods event each year on the second Saturday in September and the Midpoint Music Festival held in downtown Cincinnati each fall. There are other numerous opportunities for music in Cincinnati. They enjoy what's called Second Sunday and Final Fridays, where the music underlies these events. In their minds, the list of possibilities for music in Cincinnati is endless, and by living in an urban ecovillage, these events are close at hand.

They have seen exciting things happen here since they helped launch the ecovillage in 2004. They love being part of the CSA with a joy in gardening and the lighthearted Saturday morning food pickup, where people share successes and failures with their gardens and food preparation. For them this is a unique and valuable part of the ecovillage.

They also volunteered to help rehab a number of houses, which they do not only to help the ecovillage, but because it is fun. Some of their own interests are green technologies and the possibility of getting off the grid, which they see as being part of the future. In a way it is like the board games they love to play—a fun challenge putting the pieces together that constitutes living green. They would like to see even more educational programs offered by the ecovillage to help people make changes related to being more sustainable.

With the seriousness in making all of this happen, as they step back and look at the future of the ecovillage, they hope that the sense of play continues to expand and be reflected in all the elements of the ecovillage.

CHAPTER 12

Elders in the Ecovillage

Being in my seventies, I willingly admit, I am an elder. I have told people in the past that I did not realize my parents were getting old until they turned 70. At age 79, I have well surpassed that age. My father died in 1983 at the age of 85, my mother in 1989, at 86. As they grew older, they became a real support in our attempts at living sustainably. Though our motivations were different—theirs was survival; mine, living more sustainably—they shared a lot of information about living simply.

I still have a good deal of strength, but my stamina has waned significantly. I work with a lot of young people. The first half of the day I do fine, can keep up with them without much problem. The second half of the day finds me sitting under a tree trying to get my breath as they proceed to work the rest of the afternoon and then go off to some other activity at night. I am aging but I still look forward to experiencing the wonders of this planet for some years to come. We are "the Earth, conscious of itself," as Thomas Berry states. It is such an honor to have received this gift of Earth for a time; the opportunity to stand in awe for a while longer does appeal to me. It is out of this awe and wonder that I feel I have something to offer.

There are a significant number of people in the ecovillage who can be categorized as elders, a word I much prefer over words like senior citizens, retirees, or elderly. The world elder implies wisdom, someone who has lived a long life and learned from the experience. However, our culture sees no value in wisdom and elders are seen as a burden. Their work life is done, and they do not consume enough; also, we worry about taking care of them, of warehousing them in nursing homes and other care facilities such as dementia units. What we are doing as a culture is anything but wise; thus, elders have no real place in this culture.

However, our culture has reached a point where it needs elders to stand up and teach younger people life lessons learned. For this reason, I prefer the title Earth Elders because the most important thing we can teach younger people is that we *are* Earth and as such are intimately connected to it and totally interdependent. Elders can be integral in helping youth understand that our survival may be dependent on our awareness of our interdependence not just with Earth, not just with each other, but between our elders and our youth.

We work to apply these ideas with each other as elders in the ecovillage. We started a group that we called "Aging in Place," a common phrase these days. It soon dawned on us that the real focus of the Aging in Place movement in our culture is to figure out a way to warehouse our older population, to house them in their own homes or a home-like scenario. Our group realized that this cultural movement may be helping the aging population with housing, but what it does not do is see the value of elders for the society. Therefore, we changed our name to "Earth Elders, Aging in Place." This gives us a sense of purpose along with a focus, in this case, of continuing to live in the ecovillage.

We began our efforts by looking at our own lives and how we could enhance them. We shared the names of lawyers who could help our children avoid probate court when we die. We dealt with financial powers of attorney, living wills, and the like. While none of us enjoyed these legal matters, we knew we had to deal with them if we want to be successful in the culture. Thankfully, we spend more time talking about ways we can serve each other in the ecovillage. There are programs nationally, and specifically in Cincinnati, which provide elders with assistance in finding the services they need to keep up their homes or take care of their own personal needs. There is the "Village Movement," a program that works to create a sense of connection among elders, in addition to providing consultations for elders for any needs they have. It is a way to help elders stay in their homes and in their communities. This is a program we could see serving not only the ecovillage, but also the broader Price Hill community.

We have also looked at the notion of decluttering, making it easier for ourselves and for anyone who will come behind us after we pass. We want to make it easier for them to take care of the things that we left. Several people have decided to take this very seriously and have begun to make major steps in decluttering. One couple, primarily because of health issues, is very committed to decluttering. They come to our meetings and share humorous stories of things that seem to "disappear" from their house. He admits that he moves things out, and she admits that she hardly misses any of it. However, it is still hard for her to actually let things go. They have made huge strides, but say they still have a way to go.

The opportunity for us to communicate with each other and live closely with other elders who care about the Earth is very supportive. It helps engender a sense that being an elder is a good thing, not something to fear or resent becoming.

We used a course on Earth Eldering that five members of Imago developed a number of years ago as a way of sharing ideas for being Earth Elders called EARTH ELDERevolution. This was definitely a challenge since we have few good examples in our culture. The course provides a voice to elders via essays from people like Thomas Berry and Judith Blackburn, who have messages about being Earth Elders. Through discussion of these essays, we look at how we need to see ourselves as elders, as people who carry with us wisdom from our years of experience. And we ask ourselves how we share our Earth wisdom with the younger generations as Earth Elders.

We now start each meeting asking how we have been able to "Elder" to others during the past month. It is a great question to ask because we are not used to seeing ourselves as elders. At first, there was a good deal of hesitation as we thought about it and people would often have nothing to offer; however, as we proceed each month to answer the question, we learn from each other, and it does become easier, there is less hesitation. Now, as people observe how others interpret what they are doing as Earth Elders, there are few people who pass. It has become clear that how we live our everyday lives is the real modeling of being an Earth Elder.

My primary example of being an Earth Elder comes from working with young interns each spring through fall—one of the major ways in which I serve as an elder. I take interns through a long range of experiences, from the philosophical to the practical. I have a lot of "book learning," so I can help them understand our relationship to the Earth and the other species making up this planet. I can help them ponder an Earth-friendly relationship to an entity greater than ourselves and what that might look like.

I start the day with the interns by centering ourselves at a Medicine Wheel we have in our backyard. Into this Medicine Wheel we invite the Sun in the East, the Earth in the West. Plants and water in the South. Animals, including humans and air, in the North. In the Center we connect with the Source. Then we travel to the woods behind our house where each of us spends some time alone directly connecting with these elements. When we return, we talk about our experiences. We then each take time to write about our experiences and post them on the Community Earth Alliance blog. The blog gives the interns a chance to ground these experiences and share them with others. Once a week we watch a video of someone speaking or singing about their Earth connection and use this as a time of discussion. It is wonderful witnessing the growth and new insights the interns gain as the season progresses.

The interns split their time between working with me and working with the other elders. When they work with me, besides spending time in the woods, they may garden, clean fence rows, feed and take off the castings from worm boxes, work on the walking trail in the woods around the ecovillage, help in rehabbing a home, work at the pub, or help another resident in the ecovillage. My goal is to help them see and understand what it is like to live in a homestead in the ecovillage, as well as how the larger ecovillage functions and flourishes. This is an act of Eldering that feels right. I truly enjoy sharing the knowledge I've gained through my years of experience, as well as sharing other ideas for living sustainably.

On the other hand, the interns' youthful energy and enthusiasm is a real help to Eileen and me. They provide us with help in keeping up our own homestead. We have offered our home as a free place to stay, and those who live with us provide us with the company of young, energetic people in our home.

Serving the Ecovillage

As mentioned earlier, it is hard for older people to accept the fact that they have a lot to share, and for younger people to seek out this wisdom. We have young people saying they *want* to learn from elder wisdom, then proceed to ignore whatever is suggested by elders.

There have been some changes taking place in the ecovillage led by younger residents. The elders have talked about what is happening and feel that some of the younger residents' decisions are losing sight of the ecovillage mission and that their approach is not serving the ecovillage well. The people leading the changes insist they respect elders, but they proceed without listening to what we have to say. While it is difficult, we feel we need to give this younger leadership room to make mistakes or succeed. We acknowledge that we elders and the younger generations are all trying to learn how to elder and be eldered and to relate to one another. It is not easy.

Family

Though none of my children or grandchildren live in the eco-village, another layer of eldering comes with my relationship with my family. They are wonderful and it is exciting to be part of their lives. Watching our children make sense of their relationship to the Earth is fulfilling. They desire to be outside, walking in the woods and camping. They love being among the animals and plants they encounter while they're out among them. Eileen and I must have done something right. We love to watch our two children interact with their own children, as they help them make sense of their lives and of the planet.

While I tease, joke around, and play with my grandkids, I also take time to share my thoughts with them. I talk about our inter-connection with the Earth, that we are one of many species that are part of the planet, and how amazing that is. I have also talked to them about my sadness when some woods are cut down to build a shopping center. It is refreshing to watch them grow in their social and Earth concerns. They visit enough that I can drag them into the woods and spend time with them there. It does not take much dragging; they each love the experience.

Death

I tell my children and grandchildren about wanting to be composted when I die. While I present it in a lighthearted way, I actually do want to be interred in this way. For them this is truly unfamiliar and seems odd. They have gotten used to the idea of cremation and, recently, of green burial where a person is buried without being embalmed, without a metal casket or the grave being lined with cement. And now they are wrapping their heads around the idea that their grandfather wants to be composted. (In the state of Washington, and a number of other states, it is now legal to compost human bodies by using wood chips in a controlled facility.) In any case, this does lead them to thinking about death and dying—and also how weird their grandfather is. But I know they love me and respect me and my opinions.

Death is such a mystery that we humans have developed various and sundry ways to respond to it. Our culture spends a lot of time focusing on youth and most often deals with death by denial and avoidance. People dying around us, and our own aging bring to mind our own pending death. Our Earth Elder group tries to face it straight on because the reality is, we cannot avoid death; it will meet us at some point, with some of us earlier than with others. We talk about how we foresee our own death and reflect on the deaths of those who have gone before us.

In my own reflection, the death in the ecovillage that most impacted me was Joyce Quinlan's who lived with us intermittently a number of years over several decades. When she first lived with us, she helped us start Imago in 1978 and then left in 1980 to join a group called the Chinook Learning Center in Washington state. She had visited Chinook, and they invited her to come be a part of their programming staff. She lived there for two years and then moved to Florida where she took care of her mother for eight years. When her mother died, she returned to Cincinnati in the early 1990s. Upon her return she lived with us and worked with Imago while also getting a doctorate in Future Studies.

At 83 Joyce moved into her own home where she lived until she felt she needed more support physically in her life. She moved back to our house and lived with us for another four years. However, as her health began to deteriorate, she had increasing difficulty with balance and decided she would be better off in an assisted living facility. She left our home at the age of 92 and lived another two years in assisted living, then only a month or two in the nursing home in the same facility. She very much enjoyed the activities there and the ability to attend a Catholic mass every day, which was an important part of her life. At the age of 94 many of her systems were beginning to shut down. Close friends spent time with her as she navigated this stage of dying. She was conscious almost until the end.

Joyce had been very involved in leading Spiritual Eldering groups, a system of aging developed by Rabbi Zalman Schachter-Shalomi, author of *From Aging to Saging,* which often looked at the issue of death. Along with ways to live as an elder, he also suggested ways of planning for one's death. Joyce prepared her own funeral ritual. She had listed names and methods of reaching friends to be notified when she died. Her planning simplified her passing and allowed for the celebration of her life. We said goodbye to her in the evening, two days after she entered hospice. She died the next day, early in the morning with a friend at her side. This is an example of one person's decision on how she wanted to die, and it seemed to work very well for her and for her friends.

She is a friend we deeply miss. She had a full life and was an important person in ours by helping us found Imago and introducing us to Thomas Berry and to Rabbi Zalman Schachter-Shalomi. She provided us with a great deal of input as we began our journey to consciously connect with the Earth community. She was a close friend, living with us in our home for so many years. At that time cremation was the best ecological choice she felt she had for handling her interment. Some of her ashes are spread in Imago's labyrinth, something she helped create.

Jeanne Staas, the second really significant person to us who died, moved to the ecovillage with her husband in the 1980s. She took great care of herself; she ate well, exercised, and worked as a nurse, a job she loved. In July 2013, she was diagnosed with pancreatic cancer. This is a cancer that most times is fatal, and Jeanne was aware of this. Nevertheless, she continued to live her life with her illness. She worked at a job caring for elders, took her daily walks, came to the book club, and canned the summer and fall harvest. She was determined to live her life until she was not able to do so any longer. Toward the end of October, the illness finally took its toll and Jeanne became house-bound, then only in the last few days of life, confined to her bed. While friends visited her, she was a very private person and died in the company of her husband and nephew. She was cremated and chose not to have a special ritual around her death. Her husband was open to this. The ecovillage misses Jeanne's warmth and friendliness. She is another person who has left a hole in our lives.

The question "what happens after death" is a primary focus for most religions. Whatever the belief, the goal is to bring consolation to the one dying and also to those significant others who live on. They see their dying friend going to a better place, while also helping themselves feel solace in their own future deaths.

Those in the Earth Elder group, like most residents of the eco-village, do not have a shared idea about what happens when we die. Many people in the ecovillage belong to a spiritual tradition that gives them a suggested idea. One has a Buddha, St. Francis, an angel, and a goddess in her front yard. It always strikes me that she has all the bases covered. Regardless of our spiritual differences, most members of the ecovillage are in awe of this incredible planet we share and believe that connecting with it is a blessing. Likewise, we have a sense that we are Earth and will unite with Earth in a different way when we die.

Our Earth Elder group has discussed what we each want to do with our remains when we die. How do we do the least damage and possibly even have a positive effect on the planet? Being embalmed and buried in a coffin and vault is a terrible waste of Earth resources. It also keeps our bodies from quickly returning to become part of another element of Earth. The two people I referred to above chose to be cremated. On one level it is a much more ecological way of dealing with our bodies, but on another, the amount of energy used for cremation and the greenhouse gases it produces are concerns.

Another discussion point for our group is green burials. Until some 100 years ago, all burials were "green." There are now a few greener alternative options: burial in decomposable clothes or a shroud in a wood coffin, in a simple grave without a concrete liner and without being embalmed. This concept is just beginning to take hold. The Catholic cemetery next to the ecovillage is now performing green burials as are other cemeteries. There is now a totally green cemetery of 1000 acres in the Greater Cincinnati area that Heritage Unitarian Church recently bought for this purpose. Another new technology is the 'mushroom death suit.' The idea is that mushrooms will begin to grow from your body once it is buried, slowly digesting it, while neutralizing any environmental contaminants it may harbor, such as pesticides, heavy metals, or preservatives. The interest in what happens to the body is becoming an exciting challenge.

On my part, I hope that when the time comes, I will be in a position to accept this transition with grace. And if and when those closest to me should die, I want to be able to remember them through my continued wonder toward this planet on which we have had the honor to have stood together. My appreciation and respect for this Earth and the opportunity to be alive here and now as part of such a magnificent place, gives me the confidence that whatever happens when I die will be good and will be as it should be.

Sharon Wilson and Dennis Coskie

Growing up in Arizona, Sharon learned about geology from her grandfather, who collected stones from the desert. His message about the Earth was important to her. They lived in a remote area with snakes and scorpions, and he taught her to be mindful. She was not fearful; it was just the way it was.

She lost some of this awareness when she went to college in Ohio. At that time, the only options she saw were becoming a wife, teacher, or nurse. She decided to become a nurse. Finances were a problem. At that time, as a woman, she could not get loans for college, but nursing training was not terribly expensive, so her grandfather was able to pay for it. She is glad she became a Registered Nurse with an emphasis in psychiatric nursing. It has worked very well for her.

She met her first husband at the University of Cincinnati. Later, they moved to Rochester, New York, where their two children were born. After her husband had a number of affairs, she finally divorced him when she learned that she had breast cancer. She felt the only way she would get well was by leaving him.

Meanwhile, Dennis grew up in northern Michigan where his dad was an iron miner and his mother a housewife. He had an interest in art, so in college he studied mechanical drawing. After graduation he interviewed at Boeing Corp. On the interview tour, he saw a massive room full of desks where people were drawing, and he decided that was not how he wanted to spend his days. He went back to the university and studied industrial engineering. He liked that and graduated with a second bachelor's degree. He worked at an aerospace machine shop, then at a printing company where he moved into production management. Eventually he found a position in Chicago as vice president of operations. There he studied art, became an art collector, moved to Rochester, New York, and opened a gallery.

In a support group for separated and divorced people, Dennis met Sharon. She also had a strong interest in art, and it was one of the things that brought them together.

In the early 90s, after living on a boat in Florida for a number of years, they moved to Cincinnati where Sharon had family. After renting for several years, they began looking for a place to purchase. They wanted land and a house they could afford. Sharon took an eco-psychology course from Bill Cahalan, a founding ecovillage member, who showed the class slides of Enright Avenue and the woods around it, and they talked about simplicity. She and Dennis decided to look on Enright Avenue. They saw two houses for sale and bought the one they still live in because of the woods right beside it.

They love the amount of green space around Enright and it being just minutes from downtown Cincinnati. Before, they were driving to parks, now they live in one. Community was also attractive. As strangers, they were immediately welcomed into the neighborhood and the ecovillage.

As they have aged, they still love the opportunity to walk at the Imago Earth Center, watch sunsets over the cemetery, and share in conversations and the proverbial "cup of sugar" with their neighbors. In most neighborhoods, it is hard to know more than the people on both sides of you, but in the ecovillage, there is a much broader community of people. Their experience is that when things happen, people help each other. They believe that we need people.

They feel supported here. Sharon recently suffered from stage IV lung cancer. Through an experimental drug, she recovered, but it was a truly frightening time. On the path to recovery, people were there to help and support her and Dennis. One evening, a year after her lung cancer issue, she had to go to the hospital because of uncontrollable vomiting and severe abdominal pain. Dennis, too, was sick and could not drive her. They called 911 and when the ambulance arrived, everyone came out to be sure they were okay and to see if there was anything they could do for her or Dennis. It dawned on them that they could have asked anyone in the ecovillage or neighborhood, and someone would have driven her to the hospital.

They want to age in their own home and feel that with such amazing support from the ecovillage they will be able to do so. As elders, there are certain things they can no longer do, but there are people in the community helping them out. One neighbor mows their lawn; others look in on them and make sure that they are okay. This makes aging at home not only possible but comfortable.

Sharon and Dennis dream of the ecovillage having even more people aware and supportive of living in community and loving Earth. They see being involved with the Earth Elders, Aging in Place Committee as a way of helping to make this happen. They feel they have resources, wisdom, and compassion to share and hope to do so with even more people in the ecovillage and beyond. This gives their lives meaning and purpose.

CHAPTER 13

Celebrating Earth

I was raised in a devout Catholic family with four brothers and six sisters. Starting in grade school we began attending daily mass. Three of my sisters went to the convent. All of the boys went to the seminary to study to be priests. I entered the seminary my first year of high school and stayed for 10 years, earning both my bachelor's and a master's degree in Theology. Spirituality has been a big part of my life.

It has remained an important part of my life. In an anthology that I edited, *What Does God Look Like in an Expanding Universe?* One of the authors, John Seed, made a statement that significantly reflects my own experience. He says: "In my life there is nothing helpful about seeing anything outside the universe that is creating it. The universe itself is this single integrated activity. It does not help to think there is anything outside that is causing that to happen. Now, it could be, of course, but for me all of the miraculous things that have been attributed to any God are completely included with the universe. The universe appeared from nothing and created itself in that way. This satisfies all my hunger for the miraculous. I do not need a bigger story than that."

Seed takes the need for a transcendent God out of the equation. He basically sees the force, the power, the energy—the God— that created the universe as *within* the universe not as transcending it. I now see God in a much different light too; the notion of a God sitting on a throne up in heaven no longer makes any sense. We are in a universe that is now determined to be 93 billion light years across. If there is a God, for which there is really no proof, then God needs to encompass this massive universe. With the possibility of multiple universes, I find the notion of God truly mind boggling.

I now see God, rather than transcendent, as permeating all of creation. The best place to find this God is within this amazing planet that we are honored to be a part. For me, the best way to celebrate God is to celebrate aspects of Earth, such as the seasons, the flowers, trees, animals, the food we eat, and fellow humans.

In the Ecovillage

In the ecovillage, I would estimate that nearly all of us practice some sort of spiritual awareness in how we honor the Earth and the joy it provides. We believe that many in the larger culture have forgotten how to celebrate the wonders of this planet and this universe. We all celebrate human events: birthdays, weddings, funerals, battles, human successes, but not the wonder of the Earth and our interconnection with it. For many, this makes sense since they see the Earth as purely a resource, so there is nothing there for them to celebrate.

However, throughout the ages most humans found a spirituality, something *that which is greater than themselves* within the natural world. Most ancient religions found their gods and goddesses within the trees, the air, fire and the like. It was here that they found the mystery. In a way, John Seed's view of God is very similar, except that we can now add the new knowledge we have of Earth and universe.

In addition, there are scientists who believe that there is a genetic predisposition to our believing in *something greater than ourselves*. Geneticist Dean Hamer postulates this in his 2004 book *The God Gene: How Faith is Hardwired into our Genes*: that humans in all cultures in some way celebrate *that which is greater than themselves*. For me, this points out the innate need for humans to connect spiritually. In human history this sense of mystery changed with the advent of agriculture some 10,000 years ago; when we began domesticating animals, they no longer became sacred, which in turn, created a disconnect that made it easier to harvest them for our own needs. We can see this even more recently in the industrialization that dramatically changed the landscape of our cities and agriculture. Thus, a transcendent god was easier to work with because not seeing god within the natural world made it possible to objectify other species and the planet itself, and therefore easier to serve human needs without our feeling that we were being offensive or exploitative.

While many people in the ecovillage still participate in organized religion, they also feel the need to add the Earth dimension to their spiritual practice. Sometimes it can be found in their present religious traditions. For example, in the Catholic tradition Pope Francis, in his encyclical "Laudato Si," emphasizes the need to view the Earth in a new way based on our present knowledge of Earth and stresses the need to incorporate it within the Catholic Church celebrations. Sometimes ecovillage members include Earth celebrations in addition to their present spiritual practices. Thomas Berry, a catholic priest who became aware of the interconnectedness that we humans have within the planet, speaks of the need for us to celebrate the universe and Earth as we presently know it. Thus, we need to celebrate the Big Bang, the formation of the Sun, the formation of Earth and the other planets circling the Sun, the evolution of flowers, and evolution itself. The ecovillage has celebrated the solstice and equinox at times, though it has been organized by individuals or through

Imago. While we have not formally developed these celebrations, it is a direction I believe we may want to take as we move toward a new story of spirituality.

A New Story for the Sacred

Now in the twenty-first century, our survival needs are changing. With an awareness that we are presently damaging the planet, a new sense of the sacred is necessary. There is a need, especially at this time in history, to bring our spirituality back to Earth. While many religions have buildings that they hold as sacred, there are places within the natural world that those who celebrate Earth may hold sacred. These are places where people are able to sense their interconnectedness with Earth, with *that which is greater than oneself.* There are designated places like Stonehenge in England, Devil's Tower in Wyoming, and Ayers Rock in Australia.

But there are also parks and wooded areas; for me and many ecovillage members, we find the woods behind our homes as sacred. With two-hundred acres of woods and green space surrounding us, there is a constant celebration of Earth in the cacophony of songs, as well as competition and play among the species that live there. Humans, too, participate in this event when they enter the woods and listen and join in the life there. A well laid out trail through the woods makes it easy for humans to move gracefully among their fellow species, presenting a great opportunity to experience the oneness of Earth and of all its inhabitants. This may well be part of a new story.

In developing this new story, the celebration of Earth as primary is a key element. The celebration of Earth helps us *absorb* the new story. Our hearts sing, our feet dance, our bodies find their place in the Earth community. People who have come to understand our connection with Earth celebrate the seasons, the beauty, the awesomeness of the planet, and our interconnection with it. However, to simply follow past Earth-oriented traditions like Celtic and Native American spiritual practices is not enough. We need a *new* story for celebrating the Earth since we understand it in a new way, having gained knowledge about the Earth and the universe that was previously unknown. This knowledge can be incorporated into our celebrations.

I may be getting a little carried away with the theology of Earth celebrations, but then, I have a degree in theology, so that might be expected. You see, when I combine my early interest in theology with my greater love of Earth, I can't help but be passionate. And I feel grateful that these things can come together almost effortlessly in the ecovillage.

People in the ecovillage who care about Earth are adjusting their lives to be more in harmony with it, and many of us are using Earth celebrations as an essential part of our lives. We try to incorporate everyday things, such as walking or riding a bike rather than driving a motorized vehicle, as a way to celebrate Earth. Lowering the thermostat, using energy-efficient light bulbs, raising one's own food, cooking from scratch, planting trees, insulating houses, living and teaching others to live simply—these are all ways of celebrating Earth, celebration through action.

Earth Rituals

Thomas Berry celebrated this phenomenon. In his book *The Great Work* he says that "While the universe celebrates itself in every mode of being, the human might be identified as that being in whom the universe celebrates itself and its numinous origins in a special mode of conscious self-awareness." He speaks of celebrating such events as the big bang, the formation of stars, of planets, of evolution of plankton, and the evolution of flowers as a way our species can become aware of our connection and place in the universe.

The philosophies of Thomas Berry impact many people in our ecovillage. In addition to celebration of Earth through action, the celebration of Earth through ritual also has an important place with us. Over the years, Earth Rituals in the ecovillage have waxed and waned based on the commitment of dedicated individuals.

In the 1980s, Ruth Traut, a member of Imago, became extremely interested in rituals that honor Earth. She studied with Sun Bear, an Ojibwa author and ritualist who introduced her to Native American rituals. For close to seven years, she held Earth rituals during the full moon each month. Imago also sponsored three Medicine Wheel Gatherings in the Cincinnati area, all coordinated by Ruth. These weekend events were led by Sun Bear; he wanted to help people understand their connection to Earth and provided examples of ways to celebrate it. When Ruth moved away in the late 1980s, she left a void.

In the early 1990s, Hyemeyohsts Storm, author of *Seven Arrows*, presented a workshop for Imago. Part of it consisted of building a medicine wheel based on his directives. After this workshop we began holding a Sunday ritual: we began around the medicine wheel and then proceeded to the woods surrounding the ecovillage, where we each spent time in our own space, listening to the trees, animals, and others who made the ecosystem of the woods their home. After a time, we returned to reflect on our experiences. This continued for five years.

Over the years, Imago has held celebrations around the solstices, equinoxes, and cross quarter holidays. These have become regular since Amy, an ecovillage member, began taking on the primary responsibility for them. In these celebrations we are able to recover a sense of community with each other and with the natural world. Amy also organized a weekend retreat oriented toward the four directions for ecovillage members and others who wanted to connect with Earth in new ways. Finding the spirit that permeates the directions and air, fire, water, and earth was a central part of this retreat. Because they were held at Imago Earth Center, these celebrations also brought a sense of the sacred to the land and the Center.

There are individual families in the ecovillage who have their own Earth-centered rituals. Some families celebrate the winter solstice in a big way. Because it is the shortest day of the year, it is a time to celebrate the beginning of the return of the light. This is a much more important day for them than the traditional Christmas event because it recognizes the changes taking place between the Earth and Sun at this time of year. One family takes the four days leading up to the solstice to celebrate the four elements: air, water, earth, and fire, one each day. Then they make the day of the solstice a sacred day to celebrate. While some families will celebrate Christmas as well, others are satisfied with celebrating just the solstice.

A number of people in the ecovillage have held their weddings at the Imago Earth Center. Holding the ritual in a building and having it snuggled into the natural world is such a different experience. This setting is not seen as a backdrop to the wedding; the natural world becomes part of the ceremony. Thus, it is not only a commitment before the human community, but one before the broader community that shares space with us. This kind of marriage serves to bring the newlyweds closer to the Earth community around them.

Small rituals also happen in the ecovillage. At mealtime, some people thank the plants and animals who feed them. They do this whenever they eat, either in addition to, or rather than thanking, a transcendent god. This is a recognition of their interdependence and reverence for the non-human community that they are dependent on. It is also a way to help write the new story with celebration.

People also have rituals while gardening. For example, they explain to the plants what they are doing and why, thanking them for their lives before pulling—unearthing—them. This can be an important ritual. Could it be true that plants respected in this way are easier to pull? Thanking the plants at planting and harvest time are also important rituals for some.

One of the issues in an existing ecovillage is the place of trees. Trees are amazing plants. They provide shade for our homes; they provide a home for other species. However, they can also interfere with our human needs. They can block the sun from reaching garden areas or solar installations, or they may be in the way of building a new structure, or even in planting a more desired tree. This presents an opportunity for a ritual of thanking the tree for its life, as well as communicating with the trees around the one to be cut down and explaining to its neighbors what is happening. This is another type of ritual that helps one connect with the natural world, whether one believes that the trees actually understand or not—something I personally do.

Helping To Develop a New Story

Both formal Earth rituals and "everyday living" rituals are ways of celebrating the Earth and helping to develop the new story we need in creating a new culture. Since we have a genetic need to connect with something greater than ourselves, it is essential that the Earth and universe be a central part of this connection.

It is possible to use this and stories like it to develop a new story around our celebration of Earth and the universe. With such stories we may develop a new meaning of *that which is greater than ourselves.* With our new understandings of the Earth and universe, it is not enough to simply use ancient rituals from the past. As mentioned, we need new rituals based on the new stories we have learned about the universe and Earth. These stories, and the celebrations that evolve from them, may be what is needed at this time in history to meet our spiritual needs while helping preserve our planet. The ecovillage hopes to be part of developing this new story in its celebrations of Earth.

Celebrating Earth: Bill Cahalan

Bill grew up with a love of the natural world which was inspired by his dad. As a youth, he lived near woods and creeks and spent a lot of time outdoors, especially in the creeks, catching snakes, minnows, frogs, and turtles. He and his family grew a garden. They had many different pets; he even raised a duck as a child. However, as a teenager he was embarrassed to show that his love of nature was a passion, so he buried it until he went to college.

In 1972 several things rekindled his excitement about nature. He took a Field Studies and Natural history course, an ecology class that made him aware of our overall connection within nature. He also read the *Web of Life* by John Storer and *The Closing Circle* by Barry Commoner.

In the 1970s he became a Gestalt therapist, a form of psychotherapy based on the experiential ideal of "here and now" and relationships with others and the world, partly because it is a very earthy approach to working with people. In 1983 Bill presented a weekend retreat called "Returning to Nature and Self." To prepare for the retreat he read Wendell Berry, Theodore Roszak, Annie Dillard, and Gary Snyder for the first time. They gave him deep reflections on the disconnection from nature in our society.

Through all this, reconnecting with the natural world became a central theme for his life. In 1988 he came to Enright Avenue because he wanted to live with people who were connected to Earth. This led to his involvement in rituals, led by Ruth Traut and others, consisting of full moon rituals, seasonal celebrations, and sweat lodges.

His life on Enright eventually led him to become engaged to Deborah Jordan, who also lived in the neighborhood and who had a deep connection to Earth. They were married in 1993 and bought a house in the ecovillage. They have been steadily working to get off the grid and live more directly from the land.

For Bill, celebration or ritual grows out of the broader idea of paying attention to our connections to the natural world of plants, animals, water, air, rocks, etc. The prevailing culture is constantly and subconsciously teaching us to be disconnected and supports an individualistic, self-centered approach as workers, owners, and consumers in a technological culture. This worldview and way of life is destroying the living, breathing system of Earth. He believes that it takes an intentional daily practice, one that pays attention to our connections to the Earth within, among, and beyond us to keep us from sliding back into this technological culture.

Meditating is his most basic ritual, either sitting or walking. He meditates in a way that opens him to nature, often guided by walking. He walks a lot. Sometimes he goes off trail and tries to be conscious of the Earth he is immediately connecting with. This kind of paying attention or mindfulness, for him, is the most basic ritual of connecting to Earth.

He sometimes focuses on his breath, a very natural thing, and a direct connection to nature. He *follows* his breath, not controlling it. He opens up to the air, containing his breath and that of all creatures. Knowing that the atmosphere is maintained by the plants and animals connects him deeply to Earth. His meditation is also guided by listening to the Earth. If he hears an owl while looking out in the morning, it can lift him out of himself, a kind of out-of-body experience that sometimes connects him to the greater intelligence of Earth. He feels that what we know or experience can help deepen meditation.

However, doing rituals together with other people is also supportive and helpful. He is concerned about rituals becoming too formulated. There is a place to meet and follow a form or script, but there is also a time to be spontaneous around ritual. It is something of a paradox, how to plan a structured ritual while also including the spontaneous so that ritual does not interfere with the Mystery. As part of group rituals, he has sometimes encouraged people to tell stories about their relationship with Earth, and about their encounters with the natural world in the ecovillage.

Sometimes work becomes ritual for Bill. Working with the living landscape, getting food or firewood, building, water harvesting, turning compost, or tending the soil can be an Earth ritual. Bill wrote a paper titled "Waking Up to the Living World: Contemplative Work with the Land," and he has given workshops related to this. He feels supported by the ecovillage in doing this type of work. Working with compost among his friends and peers, doing it mindfully and intentionally, and opening to the ecosystem around them, is a ritual or celebration. It is a way of getting out of his head and sensing himself functioning as part of the land community. In fact, he believes that farming not only can be, but *needs* to be, a religious practice, as does all work.

While it is easy for so much of the work in this culture to focus on engineering or managing the Earth, he tries to do work that actually connects him with Earth. He was inspired by Wendell Berry, who began by using a tractor but decided to go back to a horse-drawn plow to get closer to the soil, touch it, and get in conversation with it, rather than being on a machine managing the land.

Bill revels in the fact that more people are interested in the ecovillage and that more ecologically minded young families are moving to it. There are more chickens and goats, more solar applications, more front yard gardens. The existence of the CSA and Common Roots are exciting to him. More people are working together with the land, gardening, and composting. All of this, for him, is a wonderful celebration of Earth.

CHAPTER 14

More of Our Stories

Matt Trokan and Merrybeth McKee

MerryBeth (MB) is the youngest of nine children. Her mother was a single mom from when she was five years old. She says they would not have survived without the help of community, namely, their church and neighbors. MB grew up in a Baltimore neighborhood of people where her mom knew everyone, and they took care of each other. This was not an intentional community, rather an old-fashioned neighborhood. Their church helped financially with a lot of things and despite several moves after MerryBeth left for college, her mother still remains in touch with many of the individuals from their church, over thirty years later. For MB, this created an appreciation for community. She had been interested in finding a community similar to what she grew up in when she learned of the ecovillage.

Because of her experiences as a young person, the idea of service is important to her. She witnessed her mom, even with very little to offer, give back to these communities whole-heartedly, with compassion and devotion. She taught her family to do the same. This, in part, has led MerryBeth to a career of service to others. She has an undergraduate degree in social work and a master's degree in public administration and currently works at an emergency shelter for children, parents, and their pets. Since she left college, she has only worked in nonprofit organizations. At one point she volunteered for "Give Back Cincinnati" and did service with them, but it was not for something she really valued. However, she found there is ample opportunity in the ecovillage where she can provide service while doing what she believes in. It is also convenient that she can offer service right in her backyard.

Matt grew up in Delhi, a community right outside of Cincinnati. His family always took camping vacations with friends. He enjoys traveling long distances by hiking or bicycle and likes to take a trip each year. He enjoys working outside, and has worked for Cincinnati City Parks, Imago Nature Center, and the US Forest Service. Two years of AmeriCorps service (where he also met MB) showed him that he could make a career out of working for nonprofits. He has a BA in history and a master's in environmental studies. He has always been an advocate for the environment. He worked for the Ohio Chapter of the Sierra Club for many years and now works at Keep Cincinnati Beautiful.

At one point, when Matt and MB lived together early on, they lived in a neighborhood where no one knew each other or communicated. They knew they did not want that. When looking for a house, they went on a tour of houses sponsored by Price Hill Will. While Matt was working at Imago, he heard about the ecovillage. He and MB were looking for community and wanted to be close to green space. They bought a house in the ecovillage that was within their price range, and it put them close to his family; he also knew people in the ecovillage from working at Imago. He worked in Lower Price Hill, which was very close by. They have been involved in the leadership of the ecovillage since 2013.

The ecovillage has been so many things for them. They got married at Imago, in the ecovillage. Because MerryBeth is an introvert and Matt is not, she created a personal challenge for herself to engage with the community when they moved in. The structure that the ecovillage provided allowed a comfortable way to participate and socialize. Despite her own hesitation, participating has always yielded a positive outcome when she goes to a public meeting or gathering.

They moved here the second year of the CSA. This has become a big anchor and also a huge carbon reducer, because it is right here in the neighborhood. It is so much easier to do the things they are doing—veggie diet, chickens, solar. They have a neighbor who opposes a lot of their practices like composting and having chickens, but they find the city, aware of what this neighborhood practices, is not so driven to push rules—like maintaining a certain distance from a property line for chickens—in ways they might if it were just an individual doing these things.

Climate change has become an important issue in their lives. They believe that climate change is happening, and that they have a responsibility to adapt and respond by living more sustainably. They believe in Thinking Globally and Acting Locally, and one of the best ways to reduce their carbon footprint is to make choices and decisions that are more sustainable in their everyday lives. This is one place where they have some control. By living more sustainably they are also healthier, happier, and in harmony with the world around them. They focus on things that are not only good for the climate but also make economic sense. These are some of the choices they have made:

- Living closer to work, which means less driving and more biking.
- Capturing solar power through solar panels lowers their utility bill.

- Developing a permaculture landscape with fruit and vegetable gardens provides them with seasonal fresh food.
- Irrigating with water from their rain barrels and gardens lowers their water bills and reduces the need to pump water to their house.
- Eating less meat is not only good for the planet but also healthier and cheaper. They grow a lot of their own food and eat most of their meals at home.
- Consuming less and recycling reduces their plastic waste.
- Keeping backyard chickens and composting take care of organic waste.

Sustainability is a lifestyle, a filter in how they make decisions in a warming world. Living in the ecovillage, closer to their friends, and within a community that supports what they are doing, is extremely helpful. The ecovillage lets them live closer to nature within the city. They do not have to travel as much because what they need and want is right here. They have learned a lot about sustainability through the ecovillage, including organic farming methods, beekeeping, backyard chickens, rain barrels, rain gardens, cob stove building, home brewing, solarization, and so much more! They have also learned that one person can have a dramatic effect, either positive or negative, on the world around them. And having people together who want to have a positive effect, has an even greater impact that radiates outward. They say it has been wonderful, in the few years they have been here, to watch the community continue to expand. There are more people and assets to build on.

Dylan Cahalan

Dylan was born in 1994 in a home birth in the house next door to where he lives now in the ecovillage with his parents. He feels fortunate that he was able to go to a Waldorf school until sixth grade. He homeschooled for seventh grade and then attended a public Montessori school through high school. He has completed college with an environmental focus and now is working at a local supermarket while determining his next step.

He likes to play sports and go hiking and biking. In his early years he had a great time playing with kids on the street: trading cards like Pokémon, playing basketball and touch football and riding bikes. He says it was great that he lived on a dead-end street which they could use as a playground. He attended the Imago summer camps and then worked as a counselor there for several summers. This was a highlight for him.

In his teenage years he felt some disillusionment with living in the ecovillage. It became obvious that the kids he had played with as a youngster did not hold the same Earth-centered values that he was developing, and so he began feeling disconnected from them. This was hard for him, though he sees that this is changing now with many new families moving to the ecovillage with young kids and similar values.

He has experienced many community-related activities over the years: potlucks, the bulk-buying club, Imago summer camps, the Music in the Woods event at Imago, and solstice rituals. There has always been a tendency toward community even with those not involved in the ecovillage. People seem to know each other better than on a typical street. He recently talked to someone who's not involved with the ecovillage but who lives here, and she expressed her appreciation for how everyone looks out for each other. One neighbor used to have a big backyard party and many neighbors would attend. There were progressive dinners and caroling for several years. Over the years he has seen the ecovillage becoming increasingly intentional with a greater number of projects and more people involved.

He finds living in the ecovillage familiar and comfortable. He feels that what is happening here, living intentionally and growing roots, is important. He is not sure that he will stay in the ecovillage, but if he does leave, he wants to be involved in building community wherever he goes. The things he finds most attractive about the ecovillage now are the easy access to woods and local organic food. He's been impressed by the harnessing of community energy that makes projects happen.

Things still are not perfect for him. There are not many people his age who have similar values living in the ecovillage. There are a good number of thirtysomethings and older and a large number of young school age kids, but not many people his age, in their twenties.

There are many things he would like to see the ecovillage undertake in the coming years. He'd love to see the development of more businesses and projects as a way to provide a living within the ecovillage. He is inspired by the example of the forestry project at Earth Haven Ecovillage, in North Carolina, where sustainable logging of the woods on their land employs many residents. The ecovillage has the CSA that employs farmers, but Dylan thinks it would be great to have other businesses as well.

For the future of the ecovillage, he anticipates new people moving here to add their skills and presence to the community. He would like to see more skill-based workshops presented by members of the ecovillage who have many skills to share. He feels it would be cool to implement a big project like large-scale solar. He thinks it could be fruitful to have a visioning time among ecovillage members to develop a lofty goal of what an ideal future might look like. He sees this as looking at how to improve what is already here and building on what is already working.

He values his upbringing and life in this urban ecovillage, and he would encourage other communities to create their own urban ecovillages.

CHAPTER 15

Things Change...and We Adapt

The Birth of Hilltop Eco-community

Much happened over the years involving backyard gardens, home rehabs, the social network, the vision, and above all, the supportive community that evolved. As part of the nonprofit, we started four businesses: Community Supported Agriculture (CSA), the pub, housing, and providing houses for rent. These provided needed resources for the ecovillage. We continued under this structure until 2019.

Even through our conflicts, the structure of the ecovillage and the board stayed consistent. The board consisted of people in the ecovillage willing to spend the time needed to carry on the organization's work. Our members served on boards and committees based on their interests and their phases in life (single, raising young children, retired, etc.) Subsequently, our board members' time and energy shifted as their lives did and as our various ecovillage projects ebbed and waned. Since the original board members were ready to pass on the proverbial baton, we were thrilled to see younger

147

families purchasing homes within the boundary of the ecovillage and expressing interest in being on the board. However, in 2019, we experienced a monumental shift.

In that year, the new board decided to take the ecovillage in a new direction. While members who had been involved with the ecovillage for years were on various committees, only three people were interested in serving on the board. At the election of board members, two people were very close for secretary, so the members decided to have two secretaries. One of them was new and the other had been on the board many years. The new president unilaterally decided to go against the decision of the members and eliminated the long-time member from the board by saying we could not have two secretaries, and he chose the one he preferred, saying she had the most votes. Another long-time ecovillage resident led the fund-raising committee on the board. However, this person and the vice president each had time conflicts regarding when the board met. The president chose the date that would keep the new member and eliminate the older member by saying the vice president position was more important than the fundraiser. Thus, two of the three were manipulated off the board. This left only me representing what we set out to do with the ecovillage back in 2004.

The newer group had a more exclusive vision: they wanted to set up a small, strongly committed ERUEV Inc. core group that would meet often and be more intentional as an inner circle followed by other tiers of membership and commitment. These tiers specified a time obligation each month and significant monetary donation to the ecovillage. Having a group strongly committed to the ecovillage seemed like a good idea. However, other changes they proposed didn't seem to fit in an ecovillage setting: 1) They decided that the boundaries of the ecovillage consisted of everyone who lived within a mile of the pub. This did not seem logical to me because they did not try to network or connect with people within this radius except for a few already involved with the ecovillage. 2) Ironically, the new board didn't think we set up the original ecovillage in a viable way, and thus they said the original Enright Ridge Urban Ecovillage wasn't an ecovillage after all. Therefore, it didn't make sense to them to work with the former leadership or any of the precedents we had set up in the nearly two decades of work we had already done. We made efforts to negotiate with them, but this proved unsuccessful.

The new ERUEV, Inc. board also decided to eliminate the established committees since they wanted to focus on just the intentional first tier of their new order of leadership. However, in the original ecovillage structure, these committees were doing most of the work in the ecovillage. One group, the EGG (Ecovillage Green Group) decided to keep working as we had, following the direction we had set up when starting the ecovillage. This group was still trying to work out a relationship with Enright Ridge Urban Ecovillage, Inc.

A number of us kept the original focus through EGG, but then the Enright Ridge Urban Ecovillage name became a bone of contention. While we founded the ecovillage and the name years before it became incorporated, the new group insisted that since they had the corporation called Enright Ridge Urban Ecovillage, Inc., they could use the name, and we could not. While we realized that we could legally continue to use the name, it wasn't worth the energy and time it would take to struggle over it. Since the Earth is in a critical time in history, we needed and wanted to focus our energy on living in a different way if our planet is to survive with humans as part of it. We don't have time to argue amongst ourselves. Even though it was sad for some of us, we decided that the best thing to do was to change our name. So, that is what we did. We are now Hilltop Eco Community. We realize that this is going to create confusion since we have promoted ERUEV for many years, but it seemed the best way to move forward without creating more conflict.

We, Hilltop Eco Community, are continuing to develop the urban ecovillage on the four streets we had been focusing on as we support each other in living more sustainably. We continue to serve as a demonstration for what neighborhoods in urban areas can do to live in harmony with the rest of the planet community.

This book refers mostly to the name Enright Ridge Urban Ecovillage, since this is the name that was used for some 15 years. We know change happens, and sometimes it's uncomfortable. Our name change does not negate the work that the current ERUEV, Inc is doing, but Hilltop Eco Community continues to focus on the four streets, welcoming new residents, being available to each other's needs, and supporting each other in living more sustainably.

Where we are today is retaining a connection to the people on the four streets. We are a small group that meets monthly. We continue to put out a monthly newsletter, set up game nights, and host potlucks. We are at a period of regrouping. Many people in the ecovillage became alienated by the conflict going on between the two groups, and while loving being part of this community are very leery of being part of a new formal structure. We are treading lightly as we move through this time.

Because we felt a need for us to work together rather than conflict, we sent a letter in August of 2022 saying:

I am writing to see if we might get together and talk. We are each a part of a group that is located in the same area, have very similar goals in terms of working to preserve this amazing planet, but approaching it in some different ways.

We really need to work out conflict so we can work together rather than just side by side. The Earth really is burning and we could do better working to preserve it if we did collaborate.

In the past we were friends that worked well together. I
must admit I much prefer that over our present estrangement.

For Earth!
Jim

We met the first part of 2023 and had a very frank but friendly discussion. They informed us that they have decided to disband as an intentional community and focus on environmental education. This was totally unexpected. At first, we worried about how this massive shift in our organization would affect the ecovillage, but we are assured that our original mission of creating community with a focus on the Earth will withstand an obstacle like this.

As mentioned in earlier chapters, not everyone who lives on the four streets in the ecovillage participates in our meetings and events. One of these long-time neighbors learned that the ecovillage was experiencing a mini crisis, and he expressed to me that "the ecovillage saved this neighborhood."

This shows that the urban retrofit ecovillage can have a positive impact on people's lives, even if they experience it on the sidelines.

Learning to live in a community is a challenge in this culture because we have forgotten how to do it. However, despite its challenges, it is still extremely rewarding to live with others who have a deep love for Earth and support each other in doing so.

There are going to be challenges. What they will look like is not known, but persistence and a strong commitment to Earth and to community can make an enormous difference to a neighborhood, make our cities more livable and more friendly to Earth.

We don't know where we will be in a year, two years, five years – but what we do know is that this ecological community will survive. People will continue to support and care for each other and for the non-human community that surrounds us. While what is happening here is not pretty, it is real and it is an example of what we can do to make cities more livable and responsive to the needs of Earth. We remain a demonstration of what we can do in our cities.

Changes Happen

Another issue with ecovillages is people changing. With the 16 people I focus on in the book, two of them have made major changes. One married couple moved to create a rural community with three other couples they knew; and one moved back to where her parents and siblings lived. On a more personal note, my wife Eileen died in 2020 due to a heart condition (not Covid). She had bypass surgery in 1990 and lived 30 more years. I am grateful for the 52 years we were married, but of course it has changed my life significantly. While I miss her, it hasn't curbed my drive to help rejuvenate the amazing planet we are a part of.

With those changes, the dynamics in the ecovillage change to some degree. People change. Every community needs to deal with this reality. There is sadness that goes with all such changes. However, because there are community and people who stay that still care deeply for each other, the community can abide these changes and still go on. This has been a huge help to me in dealing with Eileen's death. In the process, new people come and join and expand the circle.

Even with all the changes, the ecovillage, Hilltop Eco Community remains vibrant and alive. It is a wonderful place to be, where people support each other to lead lives that enhance the Earth. We have not set up another non-profit, though there is one that continues to serve us when we need it. Therefore, we don't have a board, but we have a group of people who meet monthly to give leadership to the ecovillage. We have a group that is old and young, straight and gay, a mixture of male and female. The common denominator is a love for Earth and a love for community, thus a commitment to our ecovillage. It is a wonderful place to live.

CHAPTER 16

Practical Ideas for Starting Your Urban Retrofit Ecovillage

If you have two or three households in your neighborhood who are ecologically oriented and interested in community, they may be open to starting an ecovillage. If there are not that many people with this type of interest, you may need to start recruiting eco-friendly people to move to the community. Tell people you want to set up an ecovillage and ask them to join you. There are many people out there who are interested in an ecovillage, and an urban ecovillage can be a major attraction to people who want to stay in the city. Do not be shy. Start the conversation wherever it seems plausible.

For those already living in the neighborhood, the first step is to initiate the conversation with them. You can do it individually or invite them over for dinner or snacks. Spend some time talking about why you are interested in starting an ecovillage, and then listen. If people have interest or enthusiasm, you are ready to start an ecovillage.

We started with a number of families who moved to Enright Avenue because of Imago, an ecological education organization on the street. We began with this group of people along with some other residents who were interested in ecology and community.

It is important to make sure that the people you decide to invite to the first meeting are people you trust and feel you can work with. It can become messy if someone becomes reactionary to what you are planning to do.

The First Meeting

Providing food or enjoying a potluck together is a great opportunity for people to get to know each other better. It will make the following discussion easier. This is a good time to talk together about what an ecovillage means to each person.

At our first meeting, after snacks and a chance for people to talk with each other, we started the meeting. We asked people what they would like to see in an ecovillage. We went around in the circle to make sure everyone had a chance to speak. We recorded each of their ideas. This brainstorming session gave each person a chance to express what is specific to them about an ecovillage. It brought out two pages of ideas, some of them serious, some funny, some pie in the sky—but all of them gave us a sense of what they were thinking. At the end, we clustered the items that were similar.

Next, we began seriously looking at the ideas presented. We gave everyone a set of five stars and asked them to pick out the items they felt most important to them and to put a star by those items. This gave the group a sense of what people would potentially commit to. We prioritized them according to the number of stars on the items.

We then went through the items, starting with the ones with the most stars, to see who was willing to work on it. An item may have a lot of stars, but if no one wanted to work on it, then it was set aside. Looking at the final list, we decided to start on five areas:

- Develop a hiking trail around the ecovillage - six people signed up for this committee
- Community meals - five people signed up
- Education through shared expertise - four people
- Put flowerpots with Enright Ridge Ecovillage lettered on them - five people
- Care for children on the street - four people

It's important to not overwhelm the group, but to pick things or tasks that people will actually work on. If it is only one, that's fine. If it is several, that works if there is a strong commitment. Some people will be interested in more than one thing.

Before we adjourned, each committee set up a time when they could get together and plan or actually begin working on their area. It is important that people make a commitment to each other because without it there is a chance it will not be accomplished.

At the end we talked about what people thought about the meeting. I thanked people and congratulated them on a great evening. While I would suggest setting up a second meeting date, we decided to wait and see how the committees were doing.

Second Meeting

Set a meeting in a few weeks, but not longer than a month, unless there is a good reason not to. We actually didn't meet for two months because of summer events and vacations; it was only then that we could get a majority of the people together again. As the person who initiated the idea of bringing eco-conscious people together, I took on an informal leadership role for the time being.

The groups did work on the tasks they agreed to work on. I made an effort to contact each group ahead of time to see how they were doing. Before the meeting, I sent out an agenda. The primary focus was on what each group did. I also let them know that food or snacks would be available. It is a draw for some people. We began the meeting by going around checking in on how each person was doing. We followed this by going through each of the tasks:

- Develop a hiking trail around the ecovillage: "The trail is open all around Enright Avenue. It goes through some beautiful areas. Well worth the hike."
- Community meals: "They recommended we have a potluck at the Imago Earth Center, possibly monthly. After discussion it was decided to have the first one on Sunday, September 26th."
- Education through shared expertise: No work was done on this one.
- Put flowerpots with Enright Ridge Ecovillage lettered on them: "They were installed, the flower selection wonderful, and have held up extremely well. The wording is very noticeable."
- Care for children on the street: "There continues to be problems with teens on the street. We have a real opportunity to make a positive response to the teens rather than be reactionary." Through Imago, we were able to get a Vista volunteer to work with the teens.

The second part of the meeting looked at any changes that needed to be made, then adding or subtracting tasks. Two additional task groups were recommended:

- Ways of including rest of residents on street: "The street pot-luck is one way. A second suggestion was developing a street newsletter." This was agreed to, and two people volunteered to work on this project with input and articles from others.
- Marketing Enright Ridge Urban Ecovillage as an ecovillage: "This has a potential of making Enright Avenue really special (this understanding is already floating around the city) which will improve homeownership, property values and bring people interested in the eco-village idea onto the street. Add ecovillage to the flowerpots." One of the members was a graphic designer and offered to develop a brochure.

At this meeting, we collected email addresses and started a Listserv to communicate. The next meeting was set for November 7, 2004.

Third Meeting

At our third meeting we spent time catching up on what the task groups were doing, but we also spent most of the time talking about reaching out to the rest of the neighborhood to talk to them about what we were doing. We focused on three approaches:

1. To explain how urban ecovillages have greatly improved existing neighborhoods because people who move to them take care of their houses. We talked about each of us talking to our neighbors.
2. To make it clear that people in the neighborhood are not required to do anything different because we are an ecovillage. They can choose to be involved as much as they want or not at all.

3. As mentioned before, we agreed to use the newsletter to keep people informed of what is going on; not only with our group, but about things that are going on with people in the neighborhood, such as where children are going to school, who is sick, who is traveling, or any other news about people in the ecovillage.

One of the things we could have done was develop our mission statement a little earlier. I would recommend doing this, possibly at the third meeting. It is important that people, especially those in the neighborhood, know what you are doing. We followed this definition of a mission statement: the "big-picture" intention for what the organization does. The mission statement is *internal* to the group (not external), *local* (not global), and *in the present* (not the future).

The mission statement we developed: *Enright Ridge Urban Ecovillage seeks to be an ecologically-responsible community sharing ideas, resources and a reverence for earth.*

Developing a mission statement is a great way for your group to share thoughts and ideas. It's a good way to get to know what each other thinks.

Reaching Out to the Neighborhood

We were constantly aware that we needed to reach out to the neighborhood, both to let them know what we were doing and to get them involved. In addition to the newsletter, someone suggested a process called Treasure Mapping to ask people what they would like to see in the ecovillage. We cut two sheets of 4x8-foot plywood in half and made a 4x4-foot box of four sides. We covered the four sides with sheets of paper. Based on interests expressed in our initial meetings, we labeled each side of the box: Marketing, Greening, Housing, and Family. Of course, you would need to vary these based on what is important to your ecovillage neighborhood.

We set up "ambassadors" to hand out fliers ahead of time to let people know that we wanted their input. On the day of the event, we had them go door to door when the box was near their ambassador area.

We took the box and collage-making supplies to different sections of the neighborhood: magazines, markers, crayons, scissors, glue, tape, and whatever else could be used for a collage. We asked both children and adults to make a collage around each of the four areas about what they would like to see in the ecovillage.

Following this, we invited people to come and meet with us to help decipher the collage and, in the end, to develop task force groups to work on areas that were most prominent in each area.

We reported the findings in the newsletter for those who did not come to the meeting. From what we heard, we formed committees and invited people to come and join any of the task forces with dates, times, and places of each of those gatherings. While we did not have a huge number of people join the task forces, it did serve to communicate with the entire neighborhood since two-thirds of the households participated in the Treasure Mapping.

Of course, there are other ways to reach out to the people in the neighborhood. The important thing is to make sure everyone knows what is going on. Because of this, and because we have improved the neighborhood significantly, we have no significant opposition to what we are doing.

Membership

It is important to know who is committed to being involved with the group's mission and goals. This is where membership comes in. As we developed the non-profit organization in 2006, we developed a membership process. We set a membership fee of $10 per year. Membership helped us know whom we could reach out to for help and input. When we set up the board of the non-profit organization in 2007, we set it up with all members being on the board. However, this did not work well because people didn't take their role on the board seriously. Eventually we set up an elected board of directors. We held quarterly membership meetings with the November meeting being elections of officers. This is the only time that we did 50 percent-plus-one style of voting. The rest of the board was made up of chairpersons of the committees. This resulted in almost a 100 percent attendance at the monthly board meetings.

We did not require people to be a member to be on one of the committees, though I do not remember ever having anyone on a committee who was not a member.

One of the differences between a retrofit ecovillage and a built-from-the-ground-up ecovillage is we do not have control over who lives in the community and less control over membership than those located residentially. Also, people who move or live in our community have jobs, religious practices, friends, etc., in other locations outside of the ecovillage. Because of this, the ecovillage is not generally central to their lives. It competes with all their other interests and involvements. While we would ideally like to see a deeper committment to the ecovillage, we are content with the fellowship we've established.

Setting Up a Governing Body

Some type of board or group that will give leadership is necessary, but my recommendation is to keep it as simple as possible. At the beginning, this will generally be the people who form the ecovillage. Expand it as new members join, but make sure they agree with the mission and can perform effectively with the community in mind.

We started the ecovillage with the founding members' meeting and making decisions. We set up a more formal structure in January 2005 when we set up a steering committee to guide the work in the ecovillage. The founding members chose who would be on the first steering committee.

I recommend using consensus decision making from the start. If the group is not skilled in consensus decision making, it is essential to learn about it and possibly consult with a knowledgeable person who can teach the process to your group.

Because anyone can stop the process in consensus decision making, I recommend a modified form of consensus decision making to override one or two people who disagree and block a decision, especially if a decision is necessary. Here is the way we wrote it in our by-laws:

> Section 4.4 The Board will make all decisions by consensus of those present at the meeting, with provisions for voting, if necessary. If consensus cannot be reached and a timely decision must be made, then 2/3 of the Board can call for a vote. Seventy-five percent (75%) majority vote is required to adopt the decision.

Over the years we only had one major objection or block. The person who had the objection was required to meet with the people who brought the proposal. Together they came up with an agreed-upon revision, and the revised proposal passed at the next meeting. No vote was necessary.

Set up formalized committees, with a chairperson, to work on specific projects. If you have people in the neighborhood who could help with the committee's focus, have someone who knows them well, or the chair of the committee, ask them to join. This both helps get the job done, and also begins the involvement of other people in the ecovillage effort.

Legal Structure

Unless it is necessary, I would recommend not moving too quickly to set up a legal structure. As you proceed, you can decide what type of structure would work best for your effort, which may or may not be a legal structure. Some possibilities include the following: an LLC, a cooperative, a for-profit incorporation, and a non-profit corporation. In our case, the non-profit status gave us a chance to write grants to help with projects. It might be best to work with the structure with which your leader feels the most comfortable. In our case, I knew a lot about non-profits, having been an executive director of non-profits for over 30 years. Another option is to find a non-profit that will be a financial agent for your group if you decide that non-profit would be the way for you to go.

I won't go into the other possible structures; this is something that you can research. If you do feel your organization needs a legal structure, you may find someone in the neighborhood or a friend who can give you more guidance.

* * *

I asked my friend and colleague, Diana Leafe Christian, a community consultant and author of *Creating a Life Together,* if she would add her thoughts to starting an urban retrofit ecovillage.

She adds another perspective to this discussion. While we view some items differently, looking at what we have both presented as a whole will give you a broad sweep for starting an urban retrofit ecovillage.

Diana believes founders of new communities such as urban retrofit ecovillages face a three-way Catch-22. They need to make three important decisions right at the start of their group, but each decision depends on already having made one or both of the other decisions. These are the following:

1. Choosing other founders based on their shared values and willingness to help create and support the group's shared vision and mission for the community,
2. Choosing a clear, fair, shared decision-making method with which to make these decisions, and
3. Identifying shared values and articulating a shared vision and mission.

But how can a group do this all at once?

An Added Perspective by Diana Leafe Christian

I believe the initial founder, or two or three initial founders, who'd like to create an urban retrofit ecovillage, can bypass this three-way Catch-22 like this:

First, invest the time to visit and talk with many neighbors in order to get a sense of their values, if they'd like to help create an urban retrofit ecovillage, and ideally, what activities and projects they'd like to see in the community. You could get the ball rolling in these conversations by citing the activities and projects of already existing organized neighborhoods and urban retrofit communities like Enright Ridge Urban Ecovillage; Genesee Gardens Cohousing in Lansing, Michigan; Los Angeles Eco-Village; and N Street Cohousing in Davis, California. Activities and projects like these and others could include, for example:

- Publishing a community newsletter
- Sharing meals with potlucks and/or barbeques
- Creating a childcare co-op
- Creating a pet care co-op
- Installing a neighborhood sauna
- Building a neighborhood play space for children
- Hosting game nights - for board games; skit night, movie night, storytelling night
- Cultivating one or more community gardens
- Creating a central composting project
- Encouraging public transportation by lobbying the local bus company to put a bus stop in your neighborhood
- Encouraging less car use by organizing a carpool co-op and/ or car-sharing group
- Donating books (and CDs and DVDs) to a neighborhood lending library
- Installing a basketball and/or volleyball court
- And so on.

Second, invite to the first few meetings only those neighbors who seem congenial and cooperative and whom you like, who seem to share your values, and who seem enthusiastic about projects and activities like these, and believe they will have the time to help make this happen. In addition to you (or you and two or three others whom you're starting the project with), these neighbors would constitute your founding group.

Please don't, at this early point of the process, offer an open invitation "to anyone who's interested." In my opinion, it's important to start off with people like those mentioned above, rather than with a random group of neighbors that might include those who seem overbearing and bossy, suspicious and skeptical, or even hostile to your idea to start an urban retrofit ecovillage.

At this point, having invited likely cofounders, you will have accomplished the first of the three important decisions of a new forming-community group—deciding who the founders will be: the initial group of decision-makers.

At the first meeting, ask people to choose a decision-making method that they agree to use in the first few meetings to decide the next two significant aspects of your intended community. I suggest that to help further bypass the initial Catch-22, you *don't* at this early state choose classic, traditional consensus; a modified form of consensus like the N Street Consensus Method; or sociocracy. Each of these requires paying a trainer and investing the time to learn it, including one or more people learning how to facilitate the method effectively. But right now, you just need something simple and quick to make your first decisions with people who are not already organized for the project, and who are not necessarily already skilled in consensus or sociocracy.

Rather, I suggest you choose something so simple everyone knows it: voting. The benefit is that it's easy and everyone knows how to do it. But please don't use the majority-rule voting we use for electing people to office. Majority-rule voting requires only 51 percent of people to say yes to approve a proposal and can lead to up to 49 percent feeling unhappy. Instead, I suggest creating proposals for various options, taking suggestions for improving and/or modifying the proposals, and deciding the proposals with a supermajority vote of 80 or 85 percent.

A supermajority vote requires more group members to support a proposal before it passes. This means more people in your founding group can get more of what they want, and potentially leaves fewer people feeling upset if they don't get what they want. If roughly half of the group advocated one set of projects and activities and the other half advocated several different projects and activities (or an entirely different set), the group could be stuck in an impasse, arguing back and forth about what they could or should do to launch the proposed urban retrofit ecovillage. Some could experience this as conflict in the group and quit in frustration before it even gets started.

Keep in mind that a founding group has to start *somewhere*, and just starting and deciding to move forward feels a lot better than staying stuck in limbo because the group used what they thought was a "fair" majority-rule vote. When some people feel disappointed because they didn't get what they wanted; some in the group may think, "Oh no, there's conflict in our new community!" or "Oh, but since it's *community* we are obligated to keep on discussing these issues until we can all agree, because *that's* how community functions!"

This isn't true! First, the forming group isn't a community yet. It will be someday, but right now it's just a group of people in a meeting attempting to organize what they'll be and what they'll do. And second, moving forward on the project because your supermajority voting method *allows* you to move forward is *much* more satisfying than staying stuck or arguing back and forth because you used majority-rule voting, and perhaps even disbanding from all the frustration, so no ecovillage gets started at all.

Another option for your founding group's initial decision-making choice is the "consent" method described by Ted Rau in his book *Who Decides Who Decides?* which describes how new member-led groups can launch themselves gracefully and effectively. Ted is a sociocracy trainer and the method he describes is derived from sociocracy's consent decision-making process. The consent process he recommends is a simplified version and does not require the group to learn and use all sociocracy, or even to use the entire consent decision-making method. What he suggests as the consent method is a kind of effective shortcut.

When your group chooses its initial, get-the-project-moving decision-making method, whether super-majority voting or Ted Rau's consent process, at this point you will have accomplished the second of the three important decisions of a new forming-community group.

As Jim explains in earlier chapters, I also recommend identifying your shared values and composing a paragraph or so to describe the mission of your intended urban retrofit community. After drafting the proposal wording, people will discuss and probably modify the proposal as they suggest improvements or describe their concerns and suggest ways to resolve them by offering revised wording. Then use your super-majority voting process, or Ted Rau's consent method, to approve the proposal.

Congratulations! At this point you will have accomplished the last of the three important decisions of a new community group.

However, even after you start organizing activities in the neighborhood or creating some ecovillage projects, you still have two other important issues to decide: (1) creating a membership process, and (2) choosing and getting trained in the governance and decision-making process you'll replace your simple start-up method with and use ongoingly. But at least at this point you will have the three basic tools you'll need to start your ecovillage gracefully and effectively: the members of your founding group, your simple starter decision-making method, and your shared values and intended eco-village projects and activities.

So, at a second or a third meeting of these same invited people, create a simple membership process for additional neighborhood group members. Given my years of experience on the membership committee of my own community, and in writing a book about community membership *(Finding Community)*, ideally, you'd create two kinds of ecovillage membership: regular membership and administrative membership, like this:

Regular Membership

This would be existing neighbors and people who might move to the neighborhood in order to participate in ecovillage activities, but who have less time and/or aren't so interested that they'd like to provide management and administration services like people in administrative membership *(see below)*. Regular members would be invited to participate in all ecovillage activities, social events, and work parties, and would receive the group's email notices and/or newsletter (I recommend a newsletter) about these events. They would pay no dues, unless some wanted to donate to the projects, which could be invited but voluntary.

While regular members would have no ongoing duties like administrative members, ideally, they could sit in on and observe the meetings of administrative members and make suggestions and offer opinions, but they'd have no decision-making rights in those meetings. They wouldn't have a vote if your group used super-majority voting or wouldn't be called on to give their consent if your group used Ted Rau's consent method. The fact that they'd have no decision-making authority would need to be made clear in descriptions of regular membership in ecovillage brochures, posters, the group's emails, newsletter, and/or its website (I recommend a website).

The benefit of having a regular membership—being able to participate in everything, have no regular duties and pay no dues, and not making decisions—is that by welcoming their participation in ecovillage projects, many people in your neighborhood will get to know each other far better than they otherwise would, establishing friendships, collaborations, and ideally generating more trust and harmony among neighbors than you find in regular neighborhoods. With more people knowing each other, people will most likely organize their own social gatherings, projects, and special interest groups, such as book clubs or organizing bike rides together. Your neighborhood can only benefit, experiencing more safety and neighborly cooperation, if a high number of neighbors know and interact with each other regularly.

Many regular members might later apply to become administrative members if they'd like to become more involved.

Administrative Membership

These would also be existing neighbors and people who may move to your neighborhood to participate in the ecovillage, but who are willing and able to put in the necessary time to help manage projects and make decisions. Ideally, they would be selected for congeniality, willingness to cooperate and compromise, responsibility, and the interest and time needed to help make your ecovillage happen.

Administrative members would serve as the administrative core of your project, providing management and administration services for various projects and activities. They would also pay regular dues. They would have full decision-making authority for the ecovillage, making decisions about many issues, including the following:

• Projects they'd like to see the ecovillage undertake,

- Costs for monthly (or quarterly or annual) dues they'd pay to help to fund ecovillage projects,
- Policies to help guide their work as a group,
- Guidelines for electing people for roles in administrative membership, such as meeting facilitators, a treasurer, and so on.

If the group creates a legal entity to manage the ecovillage project, administrative members will annually elect its officers and board members. If the legal entity requires a board of directors, one way to do this is to automatically make all administrative members board members. Another way is to elect board members from among all the administrative members.

Most likely people applying to become administrative members would be regular members who participate in ecovillage activities frequently enough that the administrative members get to know whether they seem congenial, cooperative, and appear to get along well with most people most of the time.

To help prevent the awful kind of "hostile takeover" that Enright Ridge Urban Ecovillage experienced, I recommend that people who apply to become administrative members would go through a screening process that includes asking for and emailing three or four character references (current or past neighbors, friends, employers, employees, housemates, and/or roommates), then sharing the responses with other administrative members. I suggest organizing a membership committee to manage the process. Ideally, there'd be an initial period in which group members could get to know the candidates for administrative membership better, assessing how willing and able they may be to participate in ecovillage activities and help make things happen.

Having two kinds of membership like this can help reduce certain kinds of conflict down the road. This is because decisions are made solely by ecovillagers who've demonstrated their commitment to the project through regular participation and willingness to pay dues, and who have a history of and reputation for congeniality, cooperation, and getting along well with most ecovillage neighbors most of the time. Specifically, this can reduce the conflict that comes when some people seem to do most of the work, and then resent people who just enjoy the benefits of community but don't actually contribute to it.

And since no one wants to "enforce" the community norm that people are expected to do some work for the ecovillage and help fund it, no one takes any action to resolve the situation. The slackers get away with it for years, generating resentment all around. Or when people who don't seem to understand the group's shared values or mission and who may not contribute much, band together in meetings to stop projects that most other community members want (by voting no or by withholding their consent), or to pass proposals to do things that stun and outrage everyone else.

I believe what happened at Enright Ridge Urban Ecovillage would not have happened if the group had had two kinds of members like this, and if administrative members who had been screened for positive qualities and who regularly contributed labor to the project made the decisions. If they had done this, I don't believe a newly elected board president could push other elected officers off the board and get away with it, as if that was a legitimate action of a board president. Or that a newly elected board decided that Enright Ridge was not and never had been an ecovillage, and no one could use that term anymore! I consider these egregious, harmful behaviors.

And at some point, in your early days, the administrative members will need to choose your ecovillage's ongoing self-governance and decision-making process to replace your simple "training wheels" process.

1. They could decide to continue using their simple super-majority voting or Ted Rau's "consent" method.

2. The administrative members could decide to get training in and thereafter use consensus, either a modified form like the N Street Method, which I highly recommend, or classic, traditional consensus, which I don't recommend anymore *(see below)*. Both forms have more aspects than super-majority voting or the consent method. The administrative members would need to hire a consensus trainer who knows and teaches the form of consensus they choose and can train one or more group members as meeting facilitators.

Why I no longer recommend classic, traditional consensus for intentional communities is because it just doesn't work. While it may work well for groups with a clearly defined issue and goal (like to save the redwoods), it tends not to work well at all in intentional communities and often creates conflict, because community living is so much more complex than a one-issue organization, as it involves everyone's daily life.

But when a community shifts from classic, traditional consensus to a modified form like my community did, people can experience the pleasure of passing their proposals and moving toward their goals, and this feels great. Being able to pass proposals, and no longer fear a proposal will be blocked for personal reasons rather than because it violates the community's mission greatly reduces tension and conflict in meetings and tends to induce much higher morale in the group as well.

3. The administrative members could decide to get training in and use sociocracy, with all its parts. These include a clear, thorough, and participatory way to create proposals; the consent decision-making method (which involves more

than the simple consent method); electing people for roles in the group; helping people perform their roles effectively with role-improvement feedback, and a clear and fair way to consider and accept new committee members or group members. Sociocracy also involves a structure of linked committees with a clear flow of information among them, and using evaluation questions to understand whether implemented proposals are working well, and if not, how to improve them.

I highly recommend sociocracy for intentional communities, even more than using a modified form of consensus, and I specialize in teaching sociocracy for communities, too.

Facilitating meetings in sociocracy is a whole lot easier because there's a step-by-step process to follow in facilitating each of its parts. There is far less pressure on the facilitator to be an exceptionally calm person with a clear mind and a great memory while also being a skilled communicator with an abundance of empathy. In sociocracy, facilitating a meeting is so much easier than facilitating consensus that regular people like you and I can facilitate a meeting easily and enjoyably.

I've seen that when communities use sociocracy effectively, they can have better meetings, get more done, become better organized, and feel more connected to other group members. However, "using sociocracy effectively," in my experience requires meeting four conditions: 1) *all* group members, not just some, learn sociocracy; 2) use all, not just some, of its parts; 3) to not combine it with consensus or voting; 4) when running into problems to get consultations or a review training from the group's sociocracy trainer. Unfortunately, when these conditions aren't met, sociocracy can work poorly and ineffectively, possibly triggering conflict.

In any case, please consider the original simple decision-making method you chose to help your group bypass the triple Catch-22 that faces new groups, as only the start-up method, the one to help your ecovillage project get started. And then do invest the time, energy, and money to get fully trained in the more useful decision-making and/or whole governance method you decide to use ongoingly. We *can* resolve the triple Catch-22 and launch urban retrofit ecovillages as successful, healthy, thriving communities.

Jim's Conclusion

These ideas are only touching the surface. There are many aspects to setting up an ecovillage. I would recommend going ahead and setting up an ecovillage in your neighborhood. It has proven to be a wonderful place to live and has drawn wonderful people to our neighborhood. Because of the demand for housing from people who want to move to the ecovillage, the urban retrofit ecovillage has the unique problem of a lack of housing for people to purchase or rent.

If you would like help in setting up your neighborhood ecovillage, feel free to contact me at jschenk@imagoearth.org or via www.communityearthalliance.org. We would love to consult with you. It is a wonderful way to live and a great way to revitalize and "green" our cities.

Resources

Urban Retrofit Ecovillages

- The Los Angeles Eco-Village neighborhood, a place name, consists of the two blocks of Bimini and White House Place in the north end of the Wilshire Center/Koreatown area of Los Angeles. https://laecovillage.org
- N Street Cohousing is a nurturing environment that offers a practical use of shared resources, cultivates personal relationships, and welcomes diversity. While there is an individual level of responsibility to the community, the community acknowledges personal choices and needs. https://nstreetcohousing.org
- Genesee Garden Cohousing is a diverse group of neighbors and friends growing a retrofit cohousing community rooted in working together, sharing resources, living with compassion and mutual respect, actively caring for our natural and social environments, embracing peace and tolerance, and promoting the health of ourselves and our wider community. https://www.facebook.com › GGCohousing

Intentional Communities References

- Global Ecovillage Network (GEN): A global network promoting sustainable communities and ecovillages: https://ecovillage.org

- Gaia Education: Provides educational programs and resources on sustainable development, including ecovillage design: https://www.gaiaeducation.org
- Foundation for Intentional Community (FIC): Provides resources, articles, and a directory of intentional communities, including ecovillages: https://www.ic.org
- Communities Magazine: Published by the Fellowship for Intentional Community, Communities Magazine explores various intentional communities, including ecovillages, cohousing, and cooperative living.
- GEN (Global Ecovillage Network) Newsletter: GEN is a global network of sustainable communities and ecovillages. Their newsletter provides updates on ecovillage projects, events, and resources.
- Books by Diana Leafe Christian
  - Creating a Life Together , Practical Tools to Grow Ecovillages and Intentional Communities
  - Finding Community, How to Join an Ecovillage or Intentional Community

Looking at Earth with New Eyes

- *The Nature Principle: Human Restoration and the End of Nature-Deficit Disorder* by Richard Louv: This book explores the healing power of nature and emphasizes the importance of reconnecting with the natural world for our well-being and spiritual growth.
- *The Hidden Life of Trees: What They Feel, How They Communicate* by Peter Wohlleben: This fascinating book delves into the secret world of trees, exploring their interconnectedness,

communication, and the lessons they can teach us about the interconnectedness of all life.

- *Nature and the Human Soul: Cultivating Wholeness and Community in a Fragmented World* by Bill Plotkin: This book offers a framework for understanding human development and the role of nature in our spiritual growth and individuation.
- *The Spell of the Sensuous: Perception and Language in a More-Than-Human World* by David Abram: This thought-provoking book explores the relationship between human perception, language, and the natural world, highlighting the sensory and spiritual dimensions of our connection with nature.
- Thomas Berry
  - *The Great Work: Our Way into the Future* (1999) - Discusses the urgent need for a transformation in human society to address the environmental crisis and offers a vision for a sustainable future.
  - Other works:
    - *The Dream of the Earth*
    - *Evening Thoughts: Reflecting on Earth as Sacred Community*
    - *The Universe Story* with Brian Swimme
  - Thomas Berry Foundation (www.thomasberry.org): The Thomas Berry Foundation was established to preserve and promote Thomas Berry's work and ideas. The website provides resources, articles, videos, and information about events and programs inspired by his teachings.

Living Simply

- *Voluntary Simplicity: Toward a Way of Life That Is Outwardly Simple, Inwardly* Rich by Duane Elgin
- *Your Money or Your Life, 9 Steps to Transforming Your Relationship with Money and Achieving Financial Independence* by Vicki Robin and Joe Dominguez
- *We Don't need Good Paying Jobs* by Jim Schenk, article at communityearthalliance.org
- Economics of Happiness: https://www.brookings.edu/wp-content/uploads/2016/06/200509.pdf
- Dolly Freed, in her book called *Possum Living: How to Live Well Without a Job and With (Almost) No Money*
- Becoming Minimalist (www.becomingminimalist.com): This website provides resources, articles, and a job board specifically focused on minimalist living and intentional simplicity.
- Simplicity Collective (www.simplicitycollective.com): This website features articles, books, and resources on living a simpler and more sustainable life, including discussions on work and employment.

Resource Sharing

- Sharing Economy Platforms: Some ecovillages participate in sharing economy platforms like Freecycle (www.freecycle.org) or Shareable (www.shareable.net), where residents can give away or lend items they no longer need and request items they require.
- Car Sharing: Ecovillagers often establish car-sharing systems where community members collectively own or share vehicles.
- Travel – home stays. There is a fee to join, the stays are free.

- https://www.couchsurfing.com/
- https://servas.org/
- The Gift Economy
- *Sacred Economics* by Charles Eisenstein - This book explores alternative economic systems, including the gift economy, and offers a thought-provoking perspective on how our current economic structures can be transformed to prioritize the well-being of individuals and communities.

Relationships

- *Beyond You and Me: Inspirations and Wisdom for Building Community* edited by Kosha Joubert, Robin Alfred, and Daniel Wahl - This anthology features contributions from various intentional communities worldwide. It covers a range of topics related to personal relationships, including communication, conflict resolution, love, and intimacy within the context of community living.
- *The Sharing Solution: How to Save Money, Simplify Your Life & Build Community* by Janelle Orsi and Emily Doskow - While not specific to intentional communities, this book explores the concept of sharing resources, including financial sharing, within a community context. It provides insights, strategies, and legal considerations for implementing sharing practices.

Housing

- Sustainable Real Estate Organizations and Networks: Connect with sustainable real estate organizations and networks that focus on eco-friendly and socially responsible property transactions. These organizations often have expertise in identifying and repurposing distressed properties for sustainable development. Examples include the Regenesis Group (www.regenesis.org) and the Green Building Alliance (gogba.org).

Decision Making

- *The Empowerment Manual: A Guide for Collaborative Groups* by Starhawk - This book explores group dynamics and decision-making within collaborative groups, including intentional communities. It offers insights, exercises, and practical tools for consensus decision-making, conflict resolution, and fostering a participatory decision-making culture.
- The ICA Group (www.ica-group.org) - The ICA Group is a nonprofit organization that provides resources and support for cooperative and community-led initiatives. Their website offers information, tools, and case studies on participatory decision-making and cooperative governance.
- *Who Decides, Who Decides? How to start a group so everyone can have a voice* by Ted J Rau – book on sociocracy

Intimacy in Ecovillages

- *Creating a Life Together: Practical Tools to Grow Ecovillages and Intentional Communities* by Diana Leafe Christian: This comprehensive guide covers various aspects of intentional community living, including relationship dynamics and managing personal boundaries. It provides practical tools and insights for fostering healthy relationships and addressing potential challenges within the community context.
- The Ecovillage.org Resource Library (www.ecovillage.org/resources): The Global Ecovillage Network's resource library offers a range of articles, reports, and case studies on different aspects of intentional community living, including managing relationships and interpersonal dynamics. It provides practical tips and advice for cultivating healthy and respectful connections within an intentional community.

Managing Challenges, Conflict Resolution

- The Empowerment Manual: A Guide for Collaborative Groups by Starhawk: This book offers practical tools and strategies for effective communication, conflict resolution, and decision-making within collaborative groups. It provides guidance on building trust, navigating power dynamics, and fostering a positive group culture.
- *Nonviolent Communication: A Language of Life* by Marshall B. Rosenberg: This book presents a framework for compassionate communication that can be valuable in resolving conflicts peacefully. It provides insights into understanding and expressing needs, active listening, and finding win-win solutions.

- The Conflict Resolution Network (www.crnhq.org): The Conflict Resolution Network offers a wide range of resources and tools on conflict resolution and mediation. Their website provides articles, online courses, and downloadable guides that can help in managing conflicts within ecovillage communities.

Living Sustainably

- Mother Earth News (www.motherearthnews.com): Provides a wide range of articles and resources on sustainable living, homesteading, and ecovillage communities.
- *The Sustainable World Radio* by Jill Cloutier: Features interviews with experts and practitioners in sustainable living, including discussions on off-grid living and ecovillage communities.
- *The Abundant Edge* by Oliver Goshey: Covers a wide range of topics related to regenerative living, permaculture, and sustainable communities, which can provide insights into off-grid living in ecovillages.
- *Living the Good Life* by Helen and Scott Nearing about their self-sufficient homesteading project in Vermont.

Families

- Parenting in Community - (www.parentingincommunity.org) provides resources and support for parents raising children in intentional communities. It offers articles, stories, and practical tips for navigating family life within a communal setting

- *Families and Communities: A View of Intentional Communities and the New Society* by David Wann: This book explores the experiences of families living in intentional communities, including ecovillages. It offers insights into the benefits, challenges, and strategies for creating a supportive environment for families within communal living settings.
- Ecovillage Family (www.ecovillagefamily.org): This website focuses specifically on supporting families in ecovillages. It offers resources, articles, and a blog that address the unique challenges and opportunities of raising children in an ecovillage setting.
- *The Unschooling Handbook: How to Use the Whole World as Your Child's Classroom* by Mary Griffith: Offers insights into unschooling, a self-directed learning approach, and how it can be applied within the context of ecovillages.
- Association of Waldorf Schools of North America (AWSNA) - www.awsna.org: Offers information about Waldorf education, resources for parents and educators, and a directory of Waldorf schools in North America.

Food

- The Organic Gardener Podcast: Features interviews with experienced gardeners, including discussions on greenhouse gardening and extending the growing season.
- *The Permaculture Handbook: Garden Farming for Town and Country* by Peter Bane: Explores permaculture principles and techniques for designing and managing sustainable gardens in various settings, including ecovillages.
- *The Small-Scale Poultry Flock: An All-Natural Approach to Raising Chickens and Other Fowl for Home and Market*

Growers by Harvey Ussery: Offers comprehensive guidance on raising chickens and other poultry in small-scale and sustainable ways.

- *Storey's Guide to Raising Dairy Goats: Breeds, Care, Dairying* by Jerry Belanger and Sara Thomson Bredesen: Provides information on raising dairy goats, including breed selection, care, and milking practices.

- *The Beekeeper's Bible: Bees, Honey, Recipes & Other Home Uses* by Richard Jones and Sharon Sweeney-Lynch: Covers various aspects of beekeeping, including hive management, honey production, and the importance of bees for ecological balance.

- National Center for Home Food Preservation (nchfp.uga.edu): Offers comprehensive information on various food preservation methods, including canning, freezing, drying, and fermenting.

- Central Ohio River Valley Guide (CORV) https://www.eatlocalcorv.org/

- The Sporkful: Hosted by Dan Pashman. This podcast covers various food-related topics, including episodes on potlucks, community meals, and shared food experiences.

- CSAs
  - *Starting Your Urban CSA, A Step-by-Step Guide to Creating a Community-Supported Agriculture Project in Your Urban Neighborhood* by Jim Schenk and Julie Hotchkiss. Read online or purchase at communityearthalliance.org/literature
  - LocalHarvest (www.localharvest.org): LocalHarvest is a comprehensive resource for finding CSAs, farmers' markets, and other local food sources in your area. They provide a directory of CSAs, information about sustainable farming practices, and educational resources.

- Biodynamic Association (www.biodynamics.com): The Biodynamic Association focuses on biodynamic farming, which emphasizes holistic and sustainable practices.
- Rodale Institute (rodaleinstitute.org): The Rodale Institute is a nonprofit organization dedicated to organic farming research and education.

Skill Sharing

- *The Sharing Economy: The End of Employment and the Rise of Crowd-Based Capitalism* by Arun Sundararajan: Explores the concept of sharing resources and skills within communities and how it can shape the future of work.

Diversity and Ecovillages

- *Building Commons and Community* by Rob Sandelin: This book explores various aspects of intentional communities, including the challenges of diversity. It addresses topics such as cultural differences, conflict resolution, and fostering inclusive decision-making processes.

Recreation and Play in the Ecovillage

- *The Art of Community: Building the New Age of Participation* by Jono Bacon: This book discusses the dynamics of community-building, including the role of work and play in fostering a vibrant and engaged community life.

Elders in Community

- *The Elder Wisdom: Crafting Your Own Elderhood* by Carol Orsborn: This book explores the concept of elderhood and offers insights into the unique contributions that elders can bring to intentional communities. It delves into topics such as wisdom, mentoring, and intergenerational relationships.
- *From Aging to Saging* by Rabbi Zalman Schachter-Shalomi looks at the important role of elders in our time.
- *Earth EldeRevolution: An Interactive Discussion Course to Re-Vision the Role of the Elder as Earth-Keeper* by Imago, Inc. Read online or purchase at communityearthalliance.org/literature.

Death

- *The Green Burial Guidebook: Everything You Need to Plan an Affordable, Environmentally Friendly Burial* by Elizabeth Fournier.
- Green Burial Council (www.greenburialcouncil.org): The Green Burial Council is an organization that promotes and sets standards for environmentally friendly burial practices. Their website provides resources, information, and a directory of green burial providers.
- Green Burial Association of Maryland (www.greenburial-maryland.org): This website provides information on green burial options in Maryland, including local providers and educational resources.
- Composting the Human Body (recompose.life): The concept of turning our dead into soil is both completely practical and deeply moving.

Celebrating Earth

- *What Does God Look Like in an Expanding Universe?* edited by Jim Schenk. Looking at our present knowledge of the universe the question is, where did we come from, why are we here and what happens after death. Go to communityearthalliance.org/literature to purchase or read the book online.
- *Seven Arrows* by Hyemeyohsts Storm. It introduces the Way of the Medicine Wheels to the modern world. https://www.universeofpoetry.org/metis.shtml
- *The Earth Path: Grounding Your Spirit in the Rhythms of Nature* by Starhawk.
- The Spiral Dance: A Rebirth of the Ancient Religion of the Great Goddess by Starhawk.
- *The Book of Ceremony: Shamanic Wisdom for Invoking the Sacred in Everyday Life* by Sandra Ingerman.
- *The Circle of Life: The Rituals of the Natural Seasons* by Joyce Rupp.

Jim Schenk has a master's degree in theology from the University of Dayton and a master's degree in social work from Case Western Reserve University. In 1978, he and his late wife Eileen founded Imago (www.imagoearth.org), an ecological education organization oriented to discovering how we would live if we held the Earth and Its people as sacred. He edited the book *What Does God Look in an Expanding Universe?* He also coauthored, with Julie Hotchkiss, the book *Starting Your Urban CSA, A Step-by-Step Guide to Creating a Community-Supported Agriculture Project in Your Urban Neighborhood.* He continues to live in the ecovillage with his partner Mary.

www.ingramcontent.com/pod-product-compliance
Lightning Source LLC
Chambersburg PA
CBHW062136040426
42335CB00038B/1218